GLASGOW
GREENS

GLASGOW GREENS

KATHRYN HAMILTON

Foreword by Marian Pallister

Neil Wilson Publishing • Glasgow • Scotland

For my family, friends, and the wee man

Published by Neil Wilson Publishing Ltd
309 The Pentagon Centre
36 Washington Street
GLASGOW G3 8AZ
Tel: 041-221-1117
Fax: 041-221-5363

A catalogue record for this book is available from the British Library.
ISBN 1-897784-11-2

Consultant editor: Derek A. Kingwell
All illustrations by McLaren and Moffat, Glasgow

Typeset in 11/12pt AvantGarde
by Face to Face Design Services, Glasgow

Printed in Musselburgh by Scotprint Ltd

CONTENTS

FOREWORD

A regular feature for some time in the *Evening Times* Saturday paper was an interview series called 'Chef's Special'. I confess it became the bane of my life! Not only did it become a hard task to find yet another new restaurant, it was also hard to elicit something new and exciting from brash young men in white hats who believed they were the best thing since Escoffier, and in fact were hard pressed to do justice in a burger bar.

I also found it increasingly frustrating as a vegetarian to covertly ask these chefs about their policies for catering for this ever-increasing minority. The answers ranged from the downright dismissive and abusive to grandiose claims about 'variety of choice' and 'innovative recipes'.

When I met Kathryn Hamilton for the series, therefore, it was as if someone had turned the light on. At that time she was getting a Glasgow city-centre restaurant off the ground and she wasn't only one of that rare breed, a vegetarian chef, but also had a wealth of recipes which really were exciting, innovative and varied.

Kathryn offered to provide not only a recipe for that week's article, but a whole series of vegetarian recipes. The opportunity to take her up on that offer came when the *Evening Times* revamped the Saturday paper. Kathryn became our vegetarian expert in residence.

Today, Glasgow is no longer a vegetarian desert. To the handful of excellent trail-blazing restaurants, including my own favourite, the Cafe Gandolfi, have been added many more where truly inventive vegetarian alternatives take their place with pride on the menu. I firmly believe that Kathryn Hamilton has been influential in the city through her work as a chef and her two-year association with the *Saturday Times.* Her recipes have been an eye-opener to me, and now sit easily within the food and drinks page in each *Saturday Times*, steadily pushing forward the frontiers to a healthy — and delicious — meat-free cuisine for a new century.

Marian Pallister
Features Editor
Saturday Times

INTRODUCTION

These are all recipes which have featured in my regular weekly column in Glasgow's *Saturday Times*. They are dishes that I have made for a crowd, for family and friends, or just myself. Some require a degree of preparation, others take literally minutes to put together and while some may include ingredients you have not used before, others incorporate those that are both basic and familiar. The common denominator is that they all make use of foods which are fresh, natural and readily available.

Vegetarian food still has a dull but worthy image clinging to it, a throwback to the brown rice, brown flour, and brown plates ethic. This is not the way I cook or eat. Over the past couple of years, meat-free cooking has changed dramatically. It has moved on to take inspiration from Mediterranean, Asian, and Eastern styles of cookery, encompassing their use of olive oils, fresh vegetables, herbs, spices, pulses, pastas, and cheeses. It is now an upmarket, cosmopolitan cuisine, where the emphasis is given to flavour and freshness, colour and texture. The wealth of fresh ingredients which fill the shelves of shops and supermarkets in abundance make it easy to create exciting, delicious and healthy dishes, without meat.

Cooking and eating should always be an enjoyable and pleasurable experience, whether alone or with company. I hope you will find the recipes which follow inspiring and exciting, and that you will enjoy using this book.

Kathryn Hamilton
July, 1994

TIPS AND TECHNIQUES

Blanching

Blanching means simply cooking vegetables briefly in boiling water, draining, and then using as required. It is a method used for skinning tomatoes, or taking the raw edge off root vegetables, particularly potatoes, carrots, parsnips, and the like.

Bread

A lot of people are put off making bread because it involves using yeast. I am no expert, but have had no disasters when using the 'easy-blend' dried yeast, which can be added directly to the flour, and makes the process very simple. To get good results, however, you should always make sure the yeast is not old, so check the 'use-by' date on the packet. Also, in most cases, bread works best when allowed to rise twice — it means the process takes longer, but the results are generally better. It is not a difficult procedure, all you need is a warm place to enable the dough to rise, then punch it down to release the air, and place it back in the warmth, leaving it to get on with rising again. Once the first few loaves have been tackled, and any initial fears dealt with, you will find it is a rewarding and enjoyable experience.

Caramelising

This is a method whereby vegetables are covered and stewed over a gentle heat in butter or oil, or a mixture of both, until they are very tender and the natural juices released have reduced and turned almost syrupy. Onions take kindly to this form of cooking, turning meltingly tender and cooking to a rich, golden brown.

Cooking spinach

Fresh spinach cooks very quickly — a huge bunch reducing to a small quantity within seconds. It cooks quite happily in the water that clings to it after washing, although a little can be added if it seems to be sticking to the pot. A lot of liquid is released, so spinach usually needs to be drained after cooking. To do this, pile the cooked spinach into a sieve or colander, and press down firmly with your hands to squeeze out excess liquid.

Filo pastry

Filo pastry makes a thin, light and crisp crust that looks impressive, but is easy to use if you follow a few guidelines:

1. Allow the pastry to defrost fully before use (2-3 hours).
2. Cool the filling slightly before assembly.
3. Make sure the filling isn't too liquidy.
4. Keep the pastry covered with a damp cloth while preparing the dish.
5. Brush the pastry well with melted butter, covering the whole surface.
6. Keep the prepared dish covered with cling film if not baking immediately.

Grilling and roasting vegetables

This is a method of cooking which works well for many vegetables, particularly peppers and aubergines, transforming their firm flesh into something that is soft and tender, and importing a gentle smokiness to their flavour.

To grill

The grill needs to be hot in order for the vegetables to cook quickly without drying out. Peppers should be halved, cored and seeded, aubergines sliced thickly. Brush the vegetables with oil, place under the hot grill (first lining the grill tray with foil), and grill until the skins of peppers are blackened and puckered, and aubergine slices are browned and tender.

To roast

The vegetables can be left whole for this method. It takes longer, and the oven needs to be really hot, above gas mark 6, 200C/400F. Brush the vegetables with oil, place on a tray and bake until the skins are browning and blistered and the vegetables are tender — this should take between 25-40 minutes.

With both methods the peppers should be placed in a bowl and covered after cooking. When cool, their skins peel easily.

Herbs

Fresh herbs are widely available all year round, and their flavour really cannot be matched. Dried herbs can be used as a substitute, but a bit of a second rate one, so whenever possible try to use fresh herbs. In most of the recipes I have given quantities for both fresh and dried, although for some there is no option given. When that is the case, use only fresh, particularly in the case of basil, parsley and coriander.

Roasting nuts

This method works best for walnuts, almonds, hazelnuts, cashews, and pecans, enriching their flavour. Spread the nuts out on a baking tray and place in a hot oven at gas mark 6, 200C/ 400F for between 5-8 minutes, until turning golden and aromatic.

Shortcrust pastry

A good, crisp crust is essential when making savoury or sweet pastry dishes. The pastry must first be partially or wholly-baked, depending on the recipe. There are a couple of techniques which help to avoid the usual shrinking of the pastry at the sides, making it impossible to add the filling without it spilling over the edges

1. Baking blind: Line a metal tart tin with the pastry, and leave to rest in the fridge for half an hour. Heat oven to gas mark 6, 200C/400F. Prick the base of the pastry, line with foil or greaseproof paper, and scatter over this dried beans or baking beans. Bake in the oven for 10 minutes, then remove the beans, foil or paper, and bake for a further 5-10 minutes for a partially baked crust, or 10-15 minutes to fully bake.

2. Baking from frozen: Line a metal tart tin with the pastry, cover lightly with foil, and place in the freezer for at least half an hour, until very firm. Prick the base of the pastry and bake from frozen in an oven preheated to gas mark 6, 200C/400F either partially for 10-15 minutes, or wholly for 20-25 minutes.

Skinning tomatoes

Fresh tomatoes need to have their skins removed before being used in sauces, stews etc. This can be done in two ways.

1. Make small slits at the stem ends of the tomatoes, place in a bowl and cover with boiling water. Leave for 1-2 minutes, until the skins have loosened. Drain, and peel the skins.
2. Again, make slits at the stem ends of the tomatoes, plunge into a pan of boiling water and blanch for 30-60 seconds. Drain and remove skins.

Toasting seeds and nuts

A simple technique, but one which adds great depth to the flavour of seeds and nuts, such as sesame, sunflower, pine nuts etc. Place the seeds or nuts in a dry pan over a gentle to medium heat, until they turn golden brown and smell 'toasty', shaking the pan to prevent the ones on the base from burning. This takes only minutes, so you need to keep an eye on them.

Vegetable stock

I have to admit I use vegetable stock cubes when it comes to soups and stews. With a few exceptions, I usually find they are good quality, and with all the other flavourings going in from the vegetables, herbs, spices etc, the stock tends to take a back seat. There are those who would frown on this, insisting that real stock cannot be matched, but I think for most of us, stock cubes provide a simple, quick alternative.

THE TRON, TRONGATE — A popular Glasgow venue, The Tron houses two bars and a theatre. The Victorian Bar offers a relaxed atmosphere and imaginative menu, with a wide variety of good vegetarian dishes.

SOUPS

Spinach and lentil soup

This soup is light and fragrant, with a delicate lemon flavour and vibrant green colour. Serve it garnished with a slice of lemon, pressing to the bottom of the bowl to release the juices.

1 tbsp olive oil
2 cloves garlic crushed
1 onion peeled and finely chopped
4 oz/115g red lentils
1 tbsp fresh rosemary, finely chopped or 2 tsp dried
1lb/450g fresh spinach, washed and chopped
     or ½ lb/225g frozen spinach, thawed and chopped
1½-2 pints/850ml-1.1 litres vegetable stock
2 tbsp lemon juice
3 tbsp natural yogurt
Salt and freshly ground black pepper

Thin slices of lemon to serve

Heat the oil in a large pan and sauté the garlic and onion until soft and translucent. Stir in the lentils and rosemary.
     Add the spinach in handfuls at a time and cook until wilted. Pour in 1½ pints/850ml of stock, cover and simmer for 15-20 minutes.
     Purée in a food processor or blender, adding more stock if the soup appears too thick. Season with salt and pepper and stir in the lemon juice and yogurt. Reheat gently before serving garnished with a slice of lemon.
     Serves 4-6.

Celeriac and pinto bean soup

Although not a particularly attractive vegetable with its gnarled and knobbly appearance, celeriac is growing in popularity and is now more widely available. Its nutty flavour adds depth to this warming soup, which is lovely for an autumn or winter meal, served with wholemeal garlic bread, or a fragrant focaccia.

1 oz/30g butter
2 tbsp olive oil
1 clove garlic, crushed
1 leek, trimmed, halved lengthways and thinly sliced
½ tsp fennel seeds
½ tsp dried marjoram
½ tsp dried basil
4 fl oz/100ml dry white wine
2 parsnips, peeled and cubed
1 good sized celeriac, trimmed, peeled and cubed
4 oz/115g mushrooms, wiped and roughly chopped
1½ pints/850ml vegetable stock
14 oz/400g canned pinto beans, drained and rinsed.
2 tbsp Greek yogurt
Salt and freshly ground black pepper

Freshly grated Parmesan cheese to serve

Heat the oil and butter in a large pan, and add the garlic and leek. Cook gently, covered, until tender. Stir in the herbs, fennel seeds, and wine, raise the heat and boil quickly until reduced. Add the vegetables, stock and beans, and bring to the boil. Reduce heat, cover, and simmer for 20-25 minutes, until vegetables are tender. Season to taste and stir in the yogurt. Reheat gently, and serve hot, sprinkled with the Parmesan cheese.
Serves 4-6.

Thai pumpkin soup

The flavours of this creamy, fragrant soup range from spicy to sweet. If pumpkin is not available, butternut squash can be used, being similar in flavour and texture. Both have wonderful orange flesh, giving this soup a vibrant, warming colour.

1 tbsp olive oil
1 oz/30g butter
1 onion or 1 red onion, peeled and finely chopped
1 clove garlic, crushed
1 red pepper, cored, seeded and diced
1½ lb/675g pumpkin, diced and weighed after trimming
  and removing skin
Juice of 1 lime, freshly squeezed
2 tomatoes, skinned and chopped
½ tsp chilli powder
2 tsp ground coriander
1 tsp ground cumin
1 pint/575ml vegetable stock
6 fl oz/175ml canned unsweetened coconut milk
Freshly gound black pepper

Finely chopped fresh coriander for garnish

Heat the oil and butter in a large, heavy based pan. Add garlic and onion and sweat together gently until translucent. Stir in the tomatoes, lime juice and spices, and sauté for a minute longer. Add the diced pepper and pumpkin, stirring to coat the pieces. Pour in the stock, bring to the boil, reduce heat, cover and simmer for 25-30 minutes until the pumpkin is tender, but not mushy. Stir in the coconut milk and season to taste. Serve as it is, or purée in a blender for a smooth soup. Serve hot, garnished with the fresh coriander.
    Serves 4-6.

Mushroom soup with pesto

This is a light soup, but the flavour is intense and full-bodied. Cultivated mushrooms can be used, but you will get a richer, earthier result by using either large, field mushrooms or the dark brown chestnut variety. It's a good spring or summer soup, served with crusty Italian or French bread.

1 oz/30g butter
1 tbsp olive oil
1 clove garlic, crushed
1 leek, trimmed and thinly sliced
1lb/450g mushrooms, wiped and sliced
1 tsp salt
1 tbsp lemon juice
2 tsp pesto
1-1½pints/575ml-850ml vegetable stock
Freshly ground black pepper

Cream or yogurt to garnish

In a large, heavy based pan, heat together the oil and butter. Add the garlic and leek, cover and sweat gently for 10 minutes, until the leek is tender. Add the mushrooms, salt and lemon juice, cover and cook gently for a further 5 minutes. Stir in 1 pint/575ml of the stock and pesto. Bring to the boil, reduce heat, cover and simmer for 25 minutes, adding more stock if you think it needs it. Remove from heat and purée in a blender. Return to the pan and reheat gently. Serve garnished with a swirl of cream or yogurt.
    Serves 4-6.

Minestrone soup

This Italian style soup is a meal in itself — thick with chunky vegetables, beans and pasta. The Parmesan cheese and herbs add wonderful fragrance and depth of flavour which gets better over time, so make it a day or two before you want to serve it.

1 onion, finely chopped
2 cloves garlic crushed
2 tbsp olive oil
8 oz/225g Savoy cabbage, shredded
1 parsnip, peeled and diced
1 carrot, peeled and diced
3 medium sized potatoes, peeled and cubed
1 red pepper, seeded, cored and diced
8 oz/225g mushrooms, wiped and sliced
6 large tomatoes, skinned and chopped or 14 oz/400g
**   canned tomatoes, chopped**
14 oz/400g canned beans drained and rinsed. Use either
**   pinto, borlotti or cannellini**
2 pints/1.1 litres vegetable stock
1 tsp each of dried basil, oregano and thyme
2 oz/55g freshly grated Parmesan cheese, plus extra for
**   serving**
2 oz/55g Tagliatelle pasta, broken
1 courgette, diced
2 tbsp fresh basil, finely chopped
Salt and freshly ground black pepper

Heat the oil in a large heavy based pan and sauté the onion and garlic until tender and translucent. Add the cabbage, parsnip, carrot, potatoes and diced pepper and continue to sauté for 5-10 minutes, stirring occasionally.

Add the mushrooms, tomatoes, stock, herbs and 2 oz/55g of the grated Parmesan cheese. Bring to the boil, reduce heat and simmer for 30 minutes. Add the beans, courgette and the pasta and continue to cook for 15-20 minutes.

Just before serving, stir in the fresh basil and season with salt and pepper. Serve sprinkled with the remaining Parmesan cheese.

Serves 6-8.

STARTERS OR LIGHT MEALS

Grilled peppers stuffed with three cheeses

This is one of my favourite combinations — tender grilled peppers, filled with a mixture of fragrant cheeses and fresh basil. It's effortless to prepare, but the end result is divine.

2 large or 3 medium peppers — use red and yellow
Olive oil or sunflower oil, for brushing
8 oz/225g Ricotta cheese
4 oz/115g goat's cheese
2 oz/55g freshly grated Parmesan cheese
1 clove garlic, crushed
2 tbsp finely chopped fresh basil
6-8 sun-dried tomatoes, packed in oil, chopped
Freshly ground black pepper

Slice peppers lengthways and remove cores and seeds. Brush with oil and place upside down under a hot grill until the skins are blackened. Remove from heat, place in a bowl and cover. For the filling, combine all the ingredients in a bowl, season with black pepper, cover and set aside. When the peppers have cooled, remove skins, and distribute filling between them. They will be very soft, so wrap in little nests of tin foil to prevent the filling oozing out. When ready to cook, place under a hot grill until the cheese is bubbling and brown. Remove the foil and serve hot on a bed of mixed salad leaves, garnished with fresh basil.
    Serves 4-6.

Sesame fried leeks with tarragon

This makes a lovely starter, vigorously flavoured, but light and delicate. All the preparation can be done in advance, but leave the frying until just before you're ready to serve them.

6 small, young leeks — white parts only, trimmed and washed
1 egg
4 oz/115g sesame seeds, lightly toasted in a pan
Olive oil for frying
Salt and freshly ground black pepper

For the vinaigrette
    2 tbsp olive oil
    1 tbsp tarragon wine vinegar
    ½ tbsp lemon juice
    ½ tsp coarse grain mustard
    1 tbsp finely chopped fresh tarragon

First make the vinaigrette by combining all the ingredients well in a bowl. Cover and set aside.

Steam the leeks for 5-8 minutes until tender — if you do not have a steamer, a metal colander set over a pan of boiling water does the job. Remove from heat and leave to cool. Beat the egg with the seasoning. Dip the leeks in the egg, coating well, then roll in the sesame seeds.

When ready to cook, heat a little olive oil in a large frying pan. When fairly hot, add the leeks and fry until golden brown — this should take about 2-3 minutes on each side.

Serve immediately on a bed of mixed lettuce leaves, drizzled with a little vinaigrette.

Serves 6 as a starter.

Cherry tomato and Ricotta tarts

These are a delicious combination of crisp, light pastry, mild creamy cheese, and colourful tomatoes. Served as individual tarts they make an attractive dish for a starter or light lunch, garnished with a little salad or a few fresh basil leaves. If you can find them, use a combination of red and yellow cherry tomatoes, which look lovely placed alternately on the filling.

12oz/350g puff pastry, thawed if frozen
1 egg, beaten, to glaze
8 oz/225g Ricotta cheese
4 oz/115g freshly grated Parmesan cheese
1 tbsp finely chopped fresh sage or 2 tsp dried
2 tbsp chopped fresh basil or 3 tsp dried
18 cherry tomatoes, halved
Freshly ground black pepper

Preheat oven to gas mark 7, 220C/425F. Roll out the pastry and line 6 small, shallow sided tart tins, about 4 inches/10cm round, pressing the pastry well up the sides. If you don't have these, you could make one large tart, using a tin about 9 inches/23cm round. Brush with the egg, prick the base, and bake in the preheated oven for 15-20 minutes until golden brown, puffy, and crisp.

For the filling, mix together the Ricotta and Parmesan cheese, stir in the herbs, and season with black pepper. Divide the filling between the cooked pastry cases, levelling the surface, and arrange the tomatoes on top, cut side down, allowing 3 for each tart. Bake for a further 10-15 minutes until the filling is hot and the tomatoes are tender. Serve hot.

Serves 6.

Stuffed avocado

The dark green Haas avocados are the best to use for this dish, as they have the toughest skins which stay intact when the flesh is scooped out. They also have the best flavour, lending richness to this summery starter. For added spices, serve with a little Salsa Harissa (see page 57) on the side.

1 small onion, finely chopped
1 clove garlic, crushed
1 tbsp olive oil
1 red or yellow pepper, cored, seeded and diced
4 oz/115g mushrooms, diced
2 stalks celery, diced
1 tbsp fresh coriander, finely chopped or 2 tsp dried
2 ripe avocados, halved lengthways and stoned
4 oz/115g Gruyère cheese, grated
2 oz/55g sunflower seeds, lightly toasted in a pan
Salt and freshly ground black pepper

Heat the oil and sauté the onion and garlic until softened. Add the pepper, mushrooms and celery and cook gently until just tender. Stir in the coriander and season. Scoop out avocado flesh being careful to leave the skin intact. Mash the flesh in a bowl, stir in the vegetable mixture and 2 oz/55g of the grated cheese.

Season to taste and pile the mixture into the avocado skins. Sprinkle with the remaining cheese and seeds. Place on a baking dish and bake in the oven gas mark 6, 200C/400F for 15-20 mins until the cheese has melted and is golden brown. Serve immediately.

Serves 4.

Aubergine with hot goat's cheese

The hot melting goat's cheese provides a soft contrast to the crunchy aubergine slices in this simple, fragrant dish. You need to use a cheese with a firm, crumbly texture in order for it to hold its shape under the grill, so try to get a French chevre, which is available in a log, from delicatessens and supermarkets. I love goat's cheese but the strong flavour and aroma is not to everyone's taste, so you could use an Italian Mozzarella instead, for an equally good but less pungent version.

1 large or 2 small aubergines, sliced about ¼ inch thick
2 eggs, beaten
2 cloves garlic, crushed
4-6 oz/115-170g wholemeal breadcrumbs
Olive oil for frying
6-8 oz/170-225g goat's cheese log — sliced into the same
**   number of slices as the aubergine**
Salt and freshly ground black pepper

Fresh basil to serve

Mix together the eggs and garlic, and season with salt and pepper. Dip the aubergine slices in the egg, then coat with the breadcrumbs. Cook the aubergines by either deep or shallow-frying in hot olive oil, until crisp and lightly browned. You will probably need to do this in batches, so keep the cooked slices warm in the oven.

Top each aubergine slice with a slice of goat's cheese and grill quickly, until the cheese is melting, bubbling and golden. Top with a fresh basil leaf and serve at once.

Serves 4-6.

Courgette and Feta fritatta

A fritatta is like a large, flat omelette, dense with vegetables and soft, melting cheese. It's good for a light summer meal, or can be left to cool and served at barbecues or picnics.

4 medium-sized courgettes, coarsely grated
2 tbsp olive oil
2 cloves garlic, crushed
6 large eggs, beaten
1 tbsp pesto or red pesto
4 oz/115g Feta cheese, diced into small cubes
4 oz/115g freshly grated Parmesan cheese
1 oz/30g butter
Salt and freshly ground black pepper

Squeeze out as much liquid from the grated courgette as possible. Heat the oil in a large, heavy based frying pan — about 9-10 ins in diameter — add the garlic and courgette and cook over a fairly high heat, stirring, until the courgette is lightly-browned and dry — about 4-5 minutes.

Remove from heat, transfer the courgette to a bowl, drain off any excess liquid, and season. Stir the cheeses and pesto into the beaten eggs, season, and stir in the courgette. Melt the butter in the frying pan, and when foaming, pour in the egg mixture.

Reduce to a very low heat, partially cover the pan, and cook gently until the eggs are almost set and the base is golden brown. Now cover the pan with a plate, invert the fritatta onto the plate, and slide back into the pan to cook the other side. Transfer the fritatta onto a serving dish, cut into wedges, and eat hot, warm or at room temperature.

Serves 4-6.

Guacamole

This is a creamy, spicy dip, fragrant with garlic and coriander. Make sure the avocados are ripe — they should give slightly when pressed — or slightly over-ripe, in order to get the best texture. It makes a nice starter or snack, served with crusty bread, slices of hot pitta bread, or tortilla chips.

3 medium sized avocados, peeled and stoned
1 small onion, peeled and finely chopped
2 cloves garlic, crushed
2 fresh chillis, seeded and very finely chopped
2 large tomatoes, skinned and chopped
Juice of 1 lemon, freshly squeezed
½ tsp finely chopped fresh coriander

Place the avocados in a bowl and mash with a fork until fairly smooth. Stir in the remaining ingredients, cover and chill until ready to serve. A good way to prevent it discolouring is to cover with cling film, allowing it to rest directly on top of the guacamole, preventing the circulation of air. However, if it does discolour slightly, just stir again before serving. The darker surface will blend in with the rest of the dip and the flavour will not be affected.
Serves 4-6.

Lentil, mushroom & walnut pâté

Served in small individual ramekins, this pâté makes a nice starter to a meal with crusty bread or oatcakes.

4 oz/115g green lentils
2 carrots, scraped and sliced
4 oz/115g mushrooms, sliced
2 oz/55g walnuts, roasted in a hot oven for 5 minutes
2 cloves garlic, crushed
1 tsp fennel seeds
1 tsp ground coriander
1 tsp oregano
2 tbsp olive oil
Lemon juice
Salt and freshly ground black pepper

Cook the lentils in plenty of boiling salted water, uncovered, for 25-30 minutes, or until soft. Drain and leave to cool. In a separate pan, boil the carrots until soft. Drain.

Heat the oil and fry the garlic, mushrooms, spices and herbs until the mushrooms are soft and just starting to release their juices.

In a large bowl, mix together the lentils, carrots, mushrooms and walnuts. Add about 1 tbsp lemon juice, transfer to a blender or food processor and blend until smooth. Season to taste, adding more lemon juice if necessary. Refrigerate until you are ready to serve.

Serves 4-6.

PECKHAMS, CLARENCE DRIVE — One of a well-established chain of popular delicatessens selling good quality cheeses, breads, preserves and wines, as well as delicious cakes and pastries.

Fried Halloumi cheese with tomato and pepper salsa

This sounds exotic, but is actually very quick and easy to pre-pare and makes an impressive but simple starter. Halloumi cheese is available from Greek or Cypriot grocers, or from some supermarkets, and has a mild, slightly salty flavour. Cooking enhances both its flavour and texture, transforming its rubbery raw origins into a cheese that is soft and light — the perfect companion for the spicy salsa.

For the salsa
  1 clove garlic, crushed
  1 yellow pepper, seeded, cored and finely chopped
  ½ red onion, peeled and finely chopped
  2 tomatoes, skinned and roughly chopped
  ½ tsp chilli powder
  2 tbsp finely chopped fresh coriander
  1 tbsp olive oil

  1 Halloumi cheese, weighing 8-10 oz/225-285g
  2-3 tbsp seasoned flour
  Olive oil for frying
  Salt and freshly ground black pepper

For the salsa

Make the salsa by combining all ingredients in a food proces-sor or blender for a few seconds until blended but still retaining some texture. Alternatively, have all the ingredients very finely chopped and combine by hand in a bowl. Cover and refriger-ate.

For the cheese

Slice into pieces about ¼ inch thick, and dip into the flour, coat-ing each side well. Heat about 1 tbsp of olive oil in a frying pan, and when it's hot, add the cheese slices to the pan. Cook for 1-2 mins on each side until golden brown.
  Serve immediately, with a spoonful of the salsa.
  Serves 4-6.

Hummous

Hummous is a Middle-eastern hors d'oeuvres made from chick peas, olive oil, lemon juice and tahini, a sesame seed paste found in health food shops and supermarkets. You can buy ready-made Hummous, but it's so quick and easy that I prefer to make it myself. It also means you can add as much garlic, olive oil, or lemon juice as you like — the end result depends very much on personal taste. Serve it as a spread, with crusty bread, or as a dip with hot pitta bread or raw vegetables, sliced into strips.

14 oz/400g canned chick peas.
2 cloves garlic, crushed
4-6 tbsp fresh lemon juice (add to taste)
2 tbsp tahini
2-4 tbsp olive oil
½ tsp ground cumin
2 dried chillis, crushed or ½ tsp chilli powder
Salt and freshly ground black pepper

Drain the chick peas and rinse them well. Using a food processor or blender, begin to purée them with garlic, until fairly smooth. Add the tahini, cumin, chilli, and some of the lemon juice and olive oil. Blend to a smooth, creamy consistency. Taste and adjust to your liking, adding more oil, garlic, or lemon juice, as necessary. Season with salt and freshly ground black pepper. Transfer to a serving bowl and refrigerate, covered, until ready to serve. It will keep for up to a week in the fridge.
Serves 4-6.

Spiced butternut pancakes

These colourful little pancakes are perfect as starters, or for a lunch or suppertime treat. Serve them freshly cooked, with sour cream or Greek yogurt.

1 large butternut squash (about 1½ lbs/675g)
2 red or green peppers, cored, seeded and finely diced
1 onion, peeled and finely chopped
3 tbsp fresh coriander, finely chopped
3-4 dried chillis, crumbled
2 oz/55g pine nuts
4 oz/115g strong Cheddar or Cheshire cheese, grated
4 eggs
2 oz/55g butter, melted
4 oz/115g plain flour
Sunflower oil for frying
Salt and freshly ground black pepper

Peel the squash and scoop out the seeds. Dice into cubes and cook in boiling water until just tender. Drain and mash. Beat eggs in a large bowl, mix in the squash and all the remaining ingredients. Season.

Heat about 1½ tbsp of oil in a frying pan. Keeping the heat fairly high, spoon 1 tbsp of the mixture per pancake into the pan, leaving space for them to spread slightly. Cook until lightly-browned, then flip over and cook the other side — allow 3-5 minutes per pancake. Transfer the cooked pancakes onto a baking tray and keep warm in the oven while you cook the remaining pancakes. When all are cooked, serve immediately.

Serves 4-6.

Stuffed mushrooms

Vegetable dishes of this kind are common throughout Italy, often with courgettes and tomatoes being stuffed in the same way. It's a very simple dish to make, but with an end result that has all the appearance and flavour of a delicacy.

6 large flat mushrooms, wiped clean
2 slices white bread, crusts removed
2 tbsp red wine
½ tbsp finely chopped fresh rosemary or 2 tsp dried
1 red pepper, halved lengthways, cored and seeded
3-4 cloves garlic, peeled
4 oz/115g freshly grated Parmesan cheese
Olive oil for brushing
Salt and freshly ground black pepper

Preheat oven to gas mark 6, 200C/ 400F. First soak the bread in the wine. Brush the pepper with oil and place under a hot grill until the skin is blistered and blackened. Remove from the grill, place in a bowl, cover and set aside.

When cool, remove skins and slice the pepper. Remove stalks from the mushrooms and place in a blender or food processor with the garlic, rosemary, Parmesan and sliced pepper.

Add seasoning then whizz until blended. Add the soaked bread, and process again to a purée. Brush the mushrooms with olive oil, fill with the stuffing, place on a baking tray, and bake in preheated oven for 25-30 mins until just tender. Serve hot.

Serves 6.

Roasted aubergine dip

The roasted aubergines give this creamy, mildly spiced dip a lovely smoky flavour. It's good either served as a spread, with crusty bread or crackers, or as a dip with crudités and breadsticks.

3 medium aubergines
2 cloves garlic, crushed
1 tbsp olive oil (more to taste)
3 tbsp natural yogurt
2 tbsp lemon juice (more to taste)
½ - 1 tsp ground cumin
Salt and freshly ground black pepper

Finely-chopped fresh coriander to garnish

Preheat oven to gas mark 6, 200C/400F. Leaving the aubergines whole, brush lightly with oil and make several slits in the skins. Place on a baking tray and bake for 35-45 mins until soft and skins are wrinkled. Remove from oven and, when cool enough to handle, chop off the stem and peel the skin.

Now purée the aubergine flesh with all the other ingredients (except the fresh coriander) until smooth and creamy. Adjust seasoning to suit adding more oil or lemon juice. Spoon into a serving dish and refrigerate for a few hours. Serve garnished with the fresh coriander.

The dip will keep for several days, covered, in the fridge.
Serves 6-8.

Grilled goat's cheese sausages

These are a variation on the more traditional Glamorgan sausages, which are made with Caerphilly cheese. Use a French goat's cheese, cut from a log, which should have a firm, crumbly texture. They are great served with a salad for a lunch or supper dish, or with scrambled eggs for a special Sunday brunch.

6 oz/170g goat's cheese (rind removed), crumbled
2 oz/55g pine nuts, lightly toasted in a pan
½ leek, finely chopped
2 tbsp finely chopped fresh coriander
5 oz/140g fresh breadcrumbs
2 eggs, beaten
1 tsp coarse grain mustard
1 egg, beaten, to coat
Extra breadcrumbs to coat
Olive oil for brushing
Salt and freshly ground black pepper

Mix the cheese with the pine nuts, leek, coriander and breadcrumbs. Beat the egg with the mustard and stir into the cheese mixture. Combine well, season with salt and freshly ground black pepper and shape in to 8-10 sausages. Dip each into the remaining beaten egg, and roll in breadcrumbs.

Chill for between 30 minutes and 1 hour. When ready to cook, brush each with olive oil, and place under a hot grill, turning frequently, until crisp and browned on each side. Serve immediately.

Makes 8-10 sausages, serving 4-5.

SALADS

Tomato and Mozzarella salad with basil and garlic

This is an attractive salad, with colours of red, green and white. It's simple, quick and effortless, but the end result depends entirely on the quality of the ingredients. Their freshness and flavour is essential, so use the best you can find.

8 ripe plum tomatoes or 4 beef tomatoes
8 oz/225g Mozzarella cheese
1 clove garlic, crushed
3 tbsp extra virgin olive oil
1 tbsp Balsamic vinegar
2 tbsp finely chopped fresh basil
Salt and freshly ground black pepper

6 sun-dried tomatoes, in oil, thinly sliced to garnish (optional)

Slice the tomatoes thinly and arrange on one large plate or four small plates. Sprinkle with a little salt, some black pepper, and the crushed garlic. Slice the Mozzarella thinly and arrange over the tomato slices. Drizzle this with the olive oil, Balsamic vinegar, and top with the chopped basil, garnishing with strips of sun-dried tomato, if using these. Add another grinding of black pepper, and serve the salad fairly soon after putting it together, to keep the flavours bright and distinct.
Serves 4.

Puy lentil salad with ginger and lime vinaigrette

Puy lentils are small black lentils, traditionally used in French cooking. They have a rustic, earthy flavour, adding depth to this dish, and contrasting well with the soft roasted peppers and creamy avocado. This is a good salad for a main meal, served warm or cold on a bed of mixed lettuce leaves, with hot crusty bread on the side.

8 oz/225g Puy lentils
1 red and 1 yellow pepper, halved lengthways, cored and
    seeded
Olive oil for brushing
2 tbsp finely chopped fresh coriander

For the dressing
    4 tbsp extra virgin olive oil
    2 tbsp white wine vinegar
    2 tsp grated fresh root ginger
    Finely grated zest and juice of 1 lime
    1 clove garlic, crushed
    2 tsp grain mustard

To serve
    2 ripe avocados, peeled, stoned and diced

Place the lentils in a pan, cover with water, bring to the boil and cook for 10 minutes. Reduce heat and simmer for 20 minutes, covered, until they are tender but still have bite and hold their shape. Drain. Brush the peppers with oil, place under a hot grill and cook until the skins are blackened and blistered. Transfer to a bowl, cover and set aside. When cool enough to handle, remove skins and slice the peppers thinly.

For the dressing, mix all the ingredients together in a bowl or jar until well combined. To assemble the salad, mix the dressing into the warm lentils, add the peppers and stir in the coriander. Taste and adjust if you think it needs it, adding more oil, vinegar or lime juice. Serve garnished with the diced avocado.
    Serves 4.

Warm potato and asparagus salad with blue cheese dressing

I have a passion for fresh asparagus, and use it as much as possible during its short season. In this salad, its presence transforms what would otherwise be a fairly ordinary dish by adding its unique delicacy of flavour. Serve as a main course, with crusty bread and green and black olives.

Approx. 8 oz/225g mixed salad leaves — use oak leaf, radicchio, rocket and cos lettuce, rinsed and dried
2 tbsp olive oil
1 clove garlic, crushed
10 oz/285g baby new potatoes, halved
8 oz/225g fresh asparagus, trimmed
2 tbsp finely chopped fresh basil
2 oz/55g fresh Parmesan cheese, sliced into shavings

For the dressing
1 clove garlic, crushed
1 egg yolk
3 oz/85g Roquefort or Stilton cheese
1 tbsp Balsamic vinegar
2 tbsp white wine vinegar
4 tbsp extra virgin olive oil

First, make the dressing by combining all the ingredients in a blender until smooth. Heat oil in a large frying pan. Add garlic and potatoes, cover and cook gently for 5 mins, stirring occasionally to prevent them from sticking. Add the asparagus, cover and sauté for 5-10 mins until both the potatoes and asparagus are tender. Arrange salad leaves on one large or four small plates. Distribute the vegetables over the leaves. Pour over dressing, then sprinkle with basil and shavings of Parmesan cheese. Serve immediately to prevent the leaves from wilting.
Serves 4.

Tabbouleh

This Middle-eastern salad is fresh and colourful, with flavours that are bright and distinct. As with most grain salads, the flavours develop as it sits, so make it a while before serving. For a main meal, serve it with hummous, some mixed lettuce leaves, and slices of hot pitta bread.

8 oz/225g bulgar wheat
4 tbsp lemon juice
3 tbsp extra virgin olive oil
6 tbsp fresh parsley, finely chopped or 3 tbsp dried
6 tbsp fresh mint, finely chopped or 3 tbsp dried
1 small cucumber
1 bunch spring onions (about 6-8)
14 oz/400g canned tomatoes, drained and finely chopped
**   or 5 large fresh tomatoes**
Salt and freshly ground black pepper

Place bulgar wheat in a bowl and pour over enough boiling water to just cover it — about ¾-1pint/450-575ml. Set aside for 15-20 mins until water has soaked in. While the wheat is soaking, prepare other ingredients. If using fresh tomatoes, make small slits at stem end, blanch in boiling water for one minute then remove skins and chop finely. Dice the cucumber and finely chop the spring onions. To assemble the salad, mix all the ingredients with the bulgar, adding more oil or lemon juice to taste. Season, cover and refrigerate.

Serve garnished with sprigs of fresh mint or parsley. The salad will keep for several days, covered, in the fridge.

Serves 4.

Couscous and vegetable salad

This is an amalgamation of tastes, mixing North African couscous with Mediterranean-style grilled vegetables, but the combination works, and the result is a colourful salad, with robust flavours, and a warm spiciness. The flavours develop the longer it sits, so make it a few hours before serving.

1 red and 1 yellow pepper, halved lengthways, cored and seeded
1 small aubergine, sliced into thick rounds
1 courgette, trimmed and halved lengthways
8 large spring onions, trimmed
Olive or sunflower oil for brushing
8 oz/225g couscous
4 tbsp finely chopped fresh coriander

For the dressing
2 tbsp extra virgin olive oil
1 tbsp white wine vinegar
Juice of 1 lemon, freshly squeezed
2 cloves garlic, crushed
1 tsp mustard — Dijon or grain
2 dried chillis, crumbled

To serve (optional)
About 3 oz/85g Feta cheese, crumbled

Brush the prepared vegetables with oil. Place under a hot grill (lined with foil), and grill until they are browned and tender. Remove from heat, transfer to a bowl and cover. Place the couscous in a bowl and pour over enough boiling water to just cover it. When the couscous has absorbed the water, rub it between your fingers to separate the grains. If it remains a little lumpy, rub in a knob of butter.

For the dressing, combine all the ingredients in a jar. When the vegetables are cool enough to handle, remove skins from the peppers. Slice all the vegetables into good sized pieces and combine with the couscous, adding any liquid from the vegetables that remains in the bowl. Stir in the dressing and coriander. Cover and set aside until ready to serve, garnished with the Feta if using this. Serve at room temperature.

Serves 4-6.

Potato salad with pesto vinaigrette

Make sure that the potatoes you use have a waxy texture, and are the tiniest you can find, leaving them whole and unpeeled to allow them to retain their earthy flavour. The dressing for this salad is bold and lively, soaking into the potatoes while they are still hot — a pleasant change from the more usual partnership with mayonnaise.

1½ lbs/675g new pototoes, scrubbed
6 spring onions, trimmed and chopped
Salt and freshly ground black pepper

For the vinaigrette
4 tbsp extra virgin olive oil
1 tbsp white wine vinegar
1 tbsp lemon juice
3-4 tsp pesto
1 clove garlic, crushed

Sprigs of Italian flat parsley to garnish

Bring a large pan of salted water to the boil, add the potatoes and cook until just tender — about 8-15 minutes, depending on size. While the potatoes are cooking, combine all the ingredients for the dressing and mix well. Taste and adjust to your liking, adding more oil, vinegar, or pesto. Drain the potatoes, place in a bowl and gently toss in the dressing while they're still hot. Cover and leave to cool, then toss again to coat in the dressing and stir in the spring onions. Serve garnished with parsley.
Serves 4-6.

GRASSROOTS, WOODLANDS ROAD — One of the best suppliers in Glasgow of wholefoods, grains, pulses, and organic produce.

Noodle salad

Adapted from a recipe by Deborah Madison, this fragrant salad has a subtle combination of oriental flavours. Served warm, on a bed of mixed lettuce leaves, it makes a colourful and aromatic dish for a light meal.

5 tbsp toasted sesame oil
5 tbsp soy sauce
2 tbsp white wine vinegar
1½-2 tbsp caster sugar
1 tsp salt
8 oz/225g packet Chinese egg noodles
2 courgettes
4 oz/115g sesame seeds
2 cloves garlic, crushed
2 tsp freshly grated root ginger (about ½ oz/15g)
Fresh coriander, finely chopped

Make the marinade by combining the oil, soy sauce, vinegar, garlic, salt and sugar in a bowl. Stir until sugar is dissolved. Bring a large pot of water to the boil and add the noodles. Cook for 3-4 minutes until done but not too soft. Drain in a colander and immediately rinse in cold water to stop any further cooking.

Shake to remove excess water, then put the noodles in a large bowl. Pour in half the marinade and mix well. Slice the courgettes in half lengthways and brush lightly with oil, then place under a hot grill and cook until the skin is just blistered. Slice into small pieces.

Toast sesame seeds in a hot pan until smelling toasty. Add the ginger to remaining marinade, gently toss the courgettes in the marinade and mix into noodles.

Add sesame seeds and mix well. Garnish with fresh coriander.

Serves 3-4.

SIDE DISHES

Roasted vegetable chips with garlic

This savoury assortment of roasted vegetable chips doesn't bear much resemblance to the more common potato chip, apart from their shape. Their texture is softer and less crispy, but the distinctive combination of flavours is delicious and makes a pleasant change. They are also lower in fat, being roasted in a small amount of olive oil. The flavours can be varied, to suit whatever you're serving them with, by adding fresh rosemary, chillis or finely chopped coriander.

2 large parsnips, peeled
2 large sweet potatoes, scrubbed
1 celeriac, peeled
4 cloves garlic, crushed
2 tbsp olive oil or sunflower oil
Salt and freshly ground black pepper

Slice the vegetables into chips about ½in/1cm thick by about 4 in/10cm long. Spread on a baking sheet and scatter over the crushed garlic. Pour over the oil and mix to coat vegetables. Bake in a hot oven, gas mark 8, 230C/450F for 30-40 minutes until lightly browned and tender. Season and serve immediately.
Serves 4.

Mushroom, mange tout and coriander ragoût

This is a dish that's simple and effortless to prepare, with a warm, pungent aroma of garlic and mushrooms which are widely available in supermarkets, with a dazzling array of names and shapes. This can be made using cultivated mushrooms, but the flavours and textures will be better if you combine several different varieties. It doesn't take to hanging around, so serve it as soon as it's ready. As a side dish, it's good with gratins, pastries, or spicy stews, or it can be served on its own for a light meal, with noodles and hot crusty bread.

1 lb/450g assorted mushrooms (use a mixture of chestnut, field, oyster and shiitake)
8 oz/225g mange tout, topped and tailed
2 cloves garlic, crushed
4 oz/115g butter
1 tbsp freshly squeezed lemon juice
2 tbsp finely chopped fresh coriander
Salt and freshly ground black pepper

Wipe the mushrooms and slice into fairly good-sized pieces. Melt the butter in a large, flat pan and add the garlic. Cook for a minute, then add the mushrooms and mange tout. Sauté over a fairly high heat for a few minutes, until the mushrooms have softened and are beginning to release their juices. Add the lemon juice and coriander, cook for another couple of minutes, and season with salt and black pepper. Serve hot.

Serves 6 as a side dish or 3-4 for a main course.

Potato cake with chives, basil and goat's cheese

All over Italy you'll find variations of this kind of vegetable dish. This is based on one eaten in the courtyard of a little family-run restaurant in the village of Barga, in Tuscany's beautiful mountainous region. The goat's cheese adds depth to the flavour and fragrance of the dish, but you could use a mild Mozzarella or creamy Ricotta instead.

2lbs/900g potatoes, peeled
4 egg yolks
2 tbsp chopped fresh chives
2 tbsp chopped fresh basil
4 oz/115g goat's cheese (rind removed), crumbled
4 oz/115g freshly grated Parmesan cheese
3 oz/85g butter
3½ oz/100g pine nuts, lightly toasted in a pan
Salt and freshly ground black pepper

Cook the potatoes in boiling salted water until tender. Drain and mash until smooth. Stir in the egg yolks, herbs, cheeses, and a little more than half of the butter. Season with salt and black pepper. With the remaining butter, use a little to grease a 9-10 inch/23-25cm round baking dish or cake tin. Use one with shallow sides, or a springform tin to make it easier to remove. Pile in the potato mixture, smoothing to a flat, level surface. Sprinkle with the pine nuts, and dot with the remaining butter. Bake in oven gas mark 6, 200C/400F, for 20-25 minutes until golden brown. Serve hot, warm, or cold, sliced into wedges.
Serves 4-6.

Spinach baked with Feta cheese and pine nuts

A typically Italian way of serving spinach, although Feta would not usually be included. However, the combination is a good one, both in terms of colour and flavour. It's a quick and simple dish to put together, and goes well alongside pastries, polenta or pastas.

1 onion, peeled and finely chopped
2 cloves garlic, crushed
2 tbsp olive oil
1 tsp dried basil
1 tsp herbes de Provence
2 lbs/900g fresh spinach, washed, stemmed and roughly
chopped
6 oz/170g Feta cheese, crumbled
3 oz/85g pine nuts, lightly toasted in a pan
4 oz/115g freshly grated Parmesan cheese
Freshly ground black pepper

Heat the oil in a large pan and add the onion and garlic. Cook gently until soft and lightly browned, then stir in the herbs. Add the spinach in handfuls at a time, cooking until just wilted. Remove from heat, stir in the Feta and season with black pepper. Transfer to a baking dish and scatter over the Parmesan and pine nuts. Bake in oven gas mark 6, 200C/400F for 20-25 mins until golden brown. Serve hot.
　　Serves 4-6.

Glazed courgettes with toasted seeds and Gruyère cheese

This is a good dish to make in the summer, when there's a glut of courgettes and they're at their best. Although made with cream, it's neither too rich or heavy, and goes well alongside a savoury tart or pasta dish.

2 tbsp olive oil
3 oz/85g butter
2 cloves garlic, crushed
6 large courgettes, wiped and sliced ¼ inch thick
1 large leek, trimmed and finely sliced
½ tbsp fresh rosemary, finely chopped
1 tbsp fresh thyme, finely chopped
10 fl oz/300ml single cream
2 oz/55g sunflower seeds, lightly toasted in a pan
4 oz/115g Gruyère cheese, grated
Salt and freshly ground black pepper

Heat the oil along with 1 oz/30g of the butter in a large pan. Add the garlic, courgettes, leek and herbs and sauté gently for a few minutes. Stir in the cream, bring to the boil, reduce heat and simmer, uncovered, until the vegetables are tender and have absorbed most of the liquid — about 15-20 mins. Season with salt and pepper.

Butter a large, shallow baking dish, pile in the vegetables, and scatter over the sunflower seeds and cheese. Dot with the remaining 2 oz/55g of butter and bake in oven gas mark 6, 200C/400F for 15-20 mins, until bubbling and golden. Serve immediately.

Serves 4-6.

Baked aubergine with Feta

This is a rich, fragrant dish which goes well alongside pastas, polenta, or savoury pastries. Here I've used red pesto, which is basil sauce made with sun-dried tomatoes. It has a warm flavour, and adds a nice deep red colour, but if it's not available ordinary pesto can be used. Either will contribute an intense flavour of basil.

2 large aubergines, sliced ¼ inch thick
6 oz/170g mushrooms, wiped and sliced
2 tbsp olive oil, plus extra for brushing
2 cloves garlic, crushed
4 large tomatoes, skinned and sliced
8 oz/225g Feta cheese, crumbled
1 tbsp red pesto
Freshly ground black pepper

Preheat oven to gas mark 6, 200C/400F. Brush the aubergine slices with oil, lay on a baking tray and bake for 10-15 mins turning once, until soft. Heat the oil, add the garlic and mushrooms and sauté over a high heat for a few minutes to just lightly cook. Spread a little pesto over the aubergine slices, and lay half of them in a lightly-oiled baking dish. Sprinkle with the mushrooms, half the Feta, and top with the remaining aubergine slices. Cover with sliced tomatoes and sprinkle with the remaining Feta. Season with black pepper and bake for 15-20 mins until hot and bubbling.
    Serves 4-6.

Spinach and sweet potato fritters

Sweet potatoes are now available from most supermarkets, and can be used in much the same way as ordinary potatoes. Here, their orange flesh adds colour, contrasting nicely with the flecks of green spinach. Serve these with a spicy stew, or as a hot accompaniment to a leafy green salad.

1lb/450g sweet potatoes, peeled and cubed
8 oz/225g new potatoes, peeled and cubed
2 egg yolks
2 oz/55g butter
1 clove garlic, crushed
1 small onion, peeled and finely chopped
8 oz/225g fresh spinach, washed, stemmed and finely
   chopped
2 oz/55g mature Cheddar, grated
1 tsp dried basil
1 egg, beaten
3-4 oz/85-115g plain flour
Olive oil for frying.
Salt and freshly ground black pepper

First cook the potatoes in boiling salted water until tender. Drain well, transfer to a bowl and mash roughly. Stir in 1oz/30g of the butter and both egg yolks. Melt remaining butter in a large pan and sauté onion and garlic until it is translucent.

Add spinach and cook quickly until just wilted. Remove from heat, drain off any excess liquid, and then mix with the potatoes. Stir in the cheese, basil, and season to taste. Shape into rounds about 3in/8cm in diameter, and leave in the fridge to firm for 30 minutes. Dip into beaten egg, then coat with flour. Heat a little oil in a pan and fry fritters over a medium heat until golden brown, about 2-3 minutes on each side. Serve hot. Makes 8-10 fritters.

Serves 4-5.

Roasted baby beetroot

Fresh beetroot has a brilliant deep purple-red colour and a robust earthy flavour which is generally lacking in its precooked counterpart. It's easy to cook and makes a wonderfully vibrant vegetable to serve with any meal.

12-16 baby beetroot, depending on available size
3 oz/85g butter
Finely grated rind of one lemon or orange
2 tbsp Balsamic or red wine vinegar
2 tbsp finely chopped fresh basil

Clean the beetroot well, being careful not to break the skin. Leave on the roots and stalks to keep the juices in, but trim if they are long. Bake in the oven at gas mark 6, 200C/400F in a single layer in a shallow amount of water, for 30-60 minutes, or until tender. Leave to cool slightly, then trim both ends and remove skins.

Melt the butter in a large, flat pan. Add the grated lemon or orange rind and the vinegar. Add the beetroot and cook for 3-5 minutes over a low heat, turning occasionally until the beet-roots are glazed.

Serve immediately, sprinkled with the fresh basil, or keep warm in the oven until ready to serve.

Serves 4-6.

ROOTS & FRUITS, GREAT WESTERN ROAD — A well-stocked fruit and veg shop selling fresh herbs, free range eggs, organic cheeses and produce ranging from the familiar to the exotic.

Cabbage baked in cream

When prepared with a bit of tender loving care, the humble cabbage can prove to be an elegant and delicious vegetable. Here it is baked with dill, cheese, and cream, making a dish that's rich in flavour and fragrance.

1 lb/450g waxy potatoes, scrubbed
1½-2 lbs/675-900g green cabbage, outer leaves removed,
    cored, quartered and thickly shredded
4 oz/115g butter
3 cloves garlic, crushed
1 tbsp fresh dill, finely chopped or 2 tsp dried dill
10 fl oz/300ml single cream
6 oz/170g Gruyère or Parmesan cheese, grated
Salt and freshly ground black pepper

Preheat oven to gas mark 6, 200C/400F. Bring a pan of salted water to the boil, add the potatoes, and cook until just tender. Drain and rinse under cold water. When cool enough to handle, cut into slices about ¼ inch thick. Melt the butter in a large, heavy based pan. Add the garlic and cabbage, in handfuls at a time, stirring to coat the cabbage in the butter. Add the dill, cover and cool gently until the cabbage is softened.

Butter a large shallow baking dish. Spoon half the cabbage over the base, and cover with the sliced potatoes, seasoning each layer with salt and pepper. Cover with the remaining cabbage. Pour over the cream, season with lots of black pepper and sprinkle with the grated cheese. Bake for 35-45 mins, until the cream is absorbed and the cheese is golden. Serve hot.

Serves 4-6.

Parsnip croquettes

These croquettes have a lovely oatmeal crust, which contrasts well with the mildly nutty flavour of the parsnips. They can be prepared in advance and kept hot in the oven until ready to serve, and are delicious with salads, stews or gratins.

2lb/900g parsnips, peeled and diced
1 oz/30g butter
2 tbsp fresh coriander, finely chopped or 1 tsp ground
 coriander
Olive oil for shallow frying
Salt and freshly ground black pepper

For the coating
 3oz/85g wholemeal flour
 2 eggs, beaten
 3 oz/85g fine oatmeal

Cook the parsnips in boiling salted water until tender for 10-15 minutes. Drain thoroughly in a colander, turn into a bowl and mash with the butter. Stir in the coriander and season with salt and pepper. Leave the mixture to cool and firm in the fridge for at least an hour. Shape into 12 croquettes.

Have ready three bowls, the first with the flour, the second with the beaten eggs, and the third with the oatmeal. Dip each croquette firstly in the flour, then the beaten egg, and then roll in the oatmeal. Flatten slightly and reshape if necessary. Heat 1 tablespoon of olive oil until fairly hot in a shallow-sided frying pan.

Depending on the size of your pan, fry 4-6 croquettes at a time for 3-4 minutes on each side until crisp and slightly browned. Keep hot in the oven while you cook the next batch. Serve hot. Makes 12 croquettes.

Serves 4-6.

SAUCES AND SALSAS

Blue cheese and basil sauce

This is a fairly rich sauce, with an intense aroma and flavour. It combines well with many dishes, such as pastas, gnocchis, or polenta. If Roquefort isn't available it can be made with Stilton or Gorgonzola, but don't add any extra salt to the sauce, since all these cheeses are quite salty in themselves.

4 oz/115g Roquefort cheese, crumbled
5 fl oz/150ml single cream
2 tbsp crème fraiche or Greek yogurt
1 tbsp finely chopped fresh basil
Freshly ground black pepper

Gently heat the cream and crème fraiche or yogurt in a pan. Stir in the basil and mix in the cheese. Stir over a gentle heat until the cheese has melted and the sauce is slightly thickened. Season with black pepper and serve hot. The sauce will keep covered in the fridge, for a few days. Makes about 7 fl oz/200ml.
  Serves 4-6.

Fresh tomato sauce

This is a simple, basic tomato sauce, but it's an essential ingredient in many dishes, particularly gratins, pastas, and with polenta. It's best made with fresh Italian plum tomatoes, as they give the richest flavour and texture. However, when stocks are low, canned tomatoes can be used instead.

2 tbsp olive oil
1 oz/30g butter
1 small onion, peeled and finely chopped
3 cloves garlic, crushed
2 lbs/900g ripe plum tomatoes, or 2 x 14oz/400g canned
    tomatoes, chopped
1 tbsp tomato purée
2 tbsp chopped fresh basil or 3 tsp dried basil
½ tsp sugar
Salt and freshly ground black pepper

First skin the tomatoes as described on page 13. Drain, peel and discard the skins and chop the tomatoes. Heat the oil and butter in a large pan, add the onion and garlic and sauté until tender. Add the tomatoes, tomato purée, basil, sugar, and seasoning.

Bring to the boil, reduce heat and simmer, uncovered, stirring ocasionally, for 15-20 minutes, until most of the liquid has evaporated and the sauce has thickened. It can be used as it is, or can be puréed in a blender or food processor. It will keep for a few days, covered in the fridge, or can be frozen. Makes about 1 pint/575ml.

Serves 4-6.

Gado gado sauce

This is a spicy Indonesian-style peanut sauce, with a rich flavour and texture. It's best served over a selection of simply prepared vegetables, such as a mixture of baby potatoes, mange tout, peppers, baby sweetcorn, mushrooms, and broccoli. Whichever ones you use, cook them until they are only just tender, so they still have a crunch to contrast with the sauce.

2 tbsp toasted sesame oil or sunflower oil
2 cloves garlic, crushed
2 onions, peeled and thinly sliced
2 oz/55gm cream of coconut, dissolved in 12 fl oz/350ml
   hot water
2 tbsp lemon juice
1 tbsp soy sauce
2 tbsp red or white wine vinegar
1 tbsp brown sugar
6 tbsp crunchy peanut butter (choose the 'no added
   sugar' type)
4 dried chillis, crumbled
1 tsp chilli powder

Heat the oil in a heavy based pan. Add the garlic and onion and sauté gently until softened. Add the remaining ingredients and cook, stirring for about 5 mins. If the sauce appears too thick, or separates, add a little more water. Serve hot.
   Serves 4-6.

Roasted red pepper and basil sauce

This deep red sauce has lovely Mediterranean flavours, intense with the aroma of roasted peppers and basil. It's particularly good with pasta or pastry dishes, or goes well with gnocchi or polenta.

4 red peppers, halved lengthways, cored and seeded
4 ripe tomatoes, skinned and chopped
½ leek, very finely chopped
2 cloves crushed garlic
2 tbsp fresh basil, chopped or 3 tsp pesto (basil sauce)
1 tbsp olive oil (plus extra for brushing)
1 oz/30g butter
Single cream
Salt and freshly ground black pepper

Heat oven to gas mark 6, 200C/400F. Brush the peppers with oil, place on a tray and bake until the skins are blistered and the peppers are tender — about 30-40 minutes. Remove from heat and place in a bowl. Cover and set aside until cool enough to handle, then peel off skins and dice the peppers. Heat the oil and butter in a pan and gently fry the garlic and leek until softened. Add the tomatoes, peppers, basil or pesto, and cook for a few more minutes. Remove from heat and purée in a blender until the sauce is smooth and glossy. Season with salt and pepper, and thin slightly with a little cream, or a little olive oil. Reheat gently before serving. Makes about ¾ pint/ 450ml.

Serves 4-6.

FRATELLI SARTI, WELLINGTON STREET — A bustling delicatessen and cafe, selling Italian cheeses, breads, olive oils, fresh pastas, and wonderful freshly-baked pizzas.

Wild mushroom and walnut sauce

This makes a rich sauce with an intense aroma. The actual mushrooms aren't used in the sauce, but don't discard them. Wipe them over to remove any grit and then add them to stews and casseroles. The sauce goes particularly well with pastas, such as cannelloni or ravioli filled with spinach.

½ oz/15g dried porcini mushrooms — available from good quality Italian delicatessens — soaked in ½ pint/300ml boiling water for 30 minutes
½ pint/300ml milk
1 oz/30g butter
1 oz/30g flour
2 oz/55g walnuts, finely chopped
1 tbsp fresh basil, finely chopped
Salt and freshly ground black pepper

Strain the stock from the mushrooms in a fine-meshed sieve. Melt the butter and stir in the flour. Cook over a gentle heat, stirring constantly, until the mixture is smooth and comes away from the sides of the pan. Remove from heat and gradually add the milk, stirring to prevent lumps from forming. Return to a gentle heat and stir until thickened.

Stir in the mushroom stock and walnuts. Season with salt and pepper, cover and simmer slowly, stirring frequently, for 20-25 mins. If the sauce appears a little thick, add a bit more stock or milk. Just before serving, stir in the fresh basil and serve hot. Makes about 1 pint/575ml.

Serves 6-8.

Salsa Harissa

I never tire of this spicy red sauce, and use it to zap up many dishes. It's good served with slices of creamy avocado, or alongside a selection of smoky grilled vegetables. Alternatively, stir a few spoonfuls into a soup or tomato sauce to add fire and flavour. Use it sparingly, since it is hot and a little goes a long way.

½ small red onion, peeled and very finely chopped.
2 cloves garlic, crushed
1 fresh red chilli, seeded and finely chopped
2 tbsp tomato purée
4 tbsp freshly squeezed lime juice
6 tbsp olive oil
1 tsp cayenne pepper
1 tbsp ground cumin
2 tbsp finely chopped fresh coriander
Salt and freshly ground black pepper

Place all the ingredients in a food processor or blender and combine until smooth and blended. Taste and adjust to your liking, adding a spot more oil and lime juice if desired. Season lightly, cover and refrigerate, where it will keep for a week or two. Makes about ½ pint/300ml.
Serves 10-12.

Salsa Verde

The flavour of this vivid green sauce can vary, according to which herbs you use and also in what quantities. It is very adaptable. Use it spread on pizzas, in baked potatoes, as a salad dressing or mix into pasta just before serving. Alternatively you can make it a dip by mixing with crème fraiche or thick, natural yogurt.

1 small onion, peeled and finely chopped
1 clove garlic, crushed
2 oz/55g parsley, finely chopped (try to use Italian flat parsley)
6 oz/170g fresh herbs, finely chopped — use a mixture of thyme, basil, dill, rocket leaves, marjoram, chervil, rosemary or tarragon
Grated rind of 1 lemon
3-4 fl oz/75-100ml extra virgin olive oil
White wine vinegar or lemon juice to taste
Salt and freshly ground black pepper

Place all the ingredients in a food processor or blender and whizz to a purée. Season and add lemon juice or vinegar to taste. Spoon into a bowl, cover and keep refrigerated. Makes about ¼ pint/150ml.

Serves 3-4.

Avocado and sun-dried tomato salsa

This spicy salsa is easily made and is good served in a number of ways. Try it with a spiced vegetable stew, or serve with hot crusty bread and a selection of cheeses and dips. The best avocados to use are the dark-skinned Haas variety, which have a buttery texture and are rich in flavour. Check for ripeness before using — the avocado should be firm but give slightly when pressed. Any that are rock hard or very soft should be avoided.

2 tomatoes, skinned and finely chopped
2 tbsp finely chopped fresh basil
6 sun-dried tomatoes (packed in oil) very finely diced
1 clove garlic, crushed
Juice of ½ lemon, freshly squeezed
1 tsp Balsamic vinegar
4 dried chillis, crumbled or 1 fresh chilli, seeded and very
finely chopped.
1 tbsp oil from the sun-dried tomatoes
1 ripe avocado, peeled, stoned and diced.

Mix together all the prepared ingredients, except the avocado. When well-combined, gently stir in the avocado. Cover and chill.
Serves 2-4.

GRATINS AND OVEN-BAKED DISHES

Potato and fennel gratin

In this dish the aniseed flavour of fennel contrasts well with the earthiness of the slowly-baked potatoes, made all the more delicious by a layer of melting cheese. Use a good quality fruity extra virgin olive oil and soft, fresh, Italian Mozzarella cheese to achieve the richest aroma and flavour.

1½ lbs/675g new potatoes, scrubbed and sliced ¼ inch
    thick
2 fennel bulbs, with the woody stalks,
    base and ends trimmed, sliced ¼ inch thick
4 plum tomatoes, blanched in boiling water, skinned and
    chopped
6 tbsp extra virgin olive oil
½ tsp dried rosemary
½ tsp dried thyme
3 crushed garlic cloves
2 onions, peeled and thinly sliced
6 oz/170g fresh Mozzarella, thinly sliced
3 oz/85g Parmesan cheese or Gruyère, grated
Salt and freshly ground black pepper

Bring a large pan of salted water to the boil and add the potatoes. Boil for five minutes then drain in a colander. Heat 2 tbsp olive oil in a large pan and add the garlic, onions, herbs, fennel and a sprinkle of salt and freshly ground black pepper.

Cook over a medium heat for a few minutes until the onions are softened. Layer the potatoes, chopped tomatoes, Mozzarella and fennel mixture in a lightly-oiled, shallow oven-proof dish, finishing with a layer of the fennel mixture.

Drizzle the remaining olive oil over the top and sprinkle with the Parmesan or Gruyère.

Bake at gas mark 6, 200C/400F covered with foil, for 30 minutes, then uncover and bake for a further 20-30 minutes or until the potatoes are tender and the cheese is bubbling and browned.

Serves 4.

Aubergine cannelloni

Tender slices of grilled aubergine are wrapped around a filling of breadcrumbs, herbs, and garlic. As it bakes, the filling soaks up the flavours and juices of the dish, intensifying in richness and aroma. This is a robust, filling dish, so serve it with a salad of mixed leaves, and chunks of hot, crusty bread.

For the filling
    3 large aubergines, trimmed and sliced lengthways,
        ¼ inch thick
    8 oz/225g fresh breadcrumbs
    3 tbsp red wine
    6 cloves garlic, crushed
    3 tbsp chopped fresh basil
    4 tbsp chopped fresh parsley
    4 oz/115g Ricotta cheese
    Salt and freshly ground black pepper

For the sauce
    2 lbs/900g tomatoes, skinned and chopped
        or 2 x 14 oz/400g cans of tomatoes, chopped
    1 onion, peeled and finely chopped
    2 cloves garlic, crushed
    2 oz/55g butter
    1 tbsp olive oil
    1 tsp dried basil

For the topping
    5 oz/140g Mozzarella, thinly sliced
    3 oz/85g freshly grated Parmesan

Brush the aubergine slices liberally with olive oil. Place under a hot grill for 5-6 mins on each side until softened and lightly browned. Set aside and leave to cool.

To make the filling, mix the breadcrumbs with the wine, lemon juice, garlic, herbs and Ricotta. Season and set aside. For the sauce, heat the oil and butter in a large pan. Add the garlic and onion, sauté until softened, then stir in the tomatoes and basil. Cover and simmer for 35-40 mins until sauce is rich and thick. Season to taste. To assemble the dish, spoon a little filling onto the aubergine slices, and fold over the aubergine, enclosing the filling. Place on a lightly-oiled, shallow-sided baking dish, keeping them tightly packed together. Pour the sauce over, covering evenly, and top with the Mozzarella and Parmesan. Bake in an oven gas mark 6, 200C/400F, for 35-40 minutes, until golden brown. Serve hot.

Serves 6.

Spinach, Parmesan and basil timbale

Baked in a light cheese and herb custard, this dish is best made with fresh spinach, which gives the best flavour and texture, but if it's not available, frozen can be used. It's a dish with lovely colours which looks attractive when unmoulded onto a plate, either in one large round, or in small individual ones. Serve it hot or warm, with a leafy mixed salad and baby potatoes roasted in olive oil.

2 lbs/900g fresh spinach or 1 lb/450g frozen
3 tomatoes, blanched, skinned and sliced
3 eggs, beaten
5 oz/140g fromage frais, or 5 oz/140g Ricotta cheese
5 fl oz/150 ml natural yogurt
1 tbsp pesto or 1 tbsp fresh basil
4 oz/115g freshly grated Parmesan cheese
Salt and freshly ground black pepper

If using frozen spinach there's no need to cook it — just thaw, squeeze out any excess water and chop it finely. If using fresh, wash it well and remove the stems. Do not dry the leaves, but place directly into a pan over a gentle heat until just wilted. Drain in a colander and squeeze out the excess water. Mix together the eggs, fromage frais or Ricotta, yogurt, basil, and season to taste. Stir in the Parmesan cheese and spinach. Butter one large, deep-sided round baking dish (or 4 small ones). Pour in half the spinach mixture, layer with the sliced tomatoes, and top with the remaining spinach.

Bake at gas mark 4, 180C/350F for 45 mins to 1 hour, or until firm to touch and lightly browned. Leave to cool for a few minutes, then slide a flat pallet knife round the edges and carefully place upside down onto a serving plate. Tap the base gently and lift free.

Serves 4.

Stuffed butternut squash

Butternut squash have a bulbous shape and vibrant orange flesh. In this dish, the character of both is retained, making it one that is not only delicious, but also visually attractive. They are now a common sight in major supermarkets, seeming to be available throughout most of the seasons. Serve this with a spoonful of Salsa Verde (see page 58), which complements both the colour and flavour of the squash.

2 butternut squash halved lengthways, seeds and fibres removed
Oil for brushing
2 oz/55g butter
2 cloves garlic, crushed
8 oz/225g mushrooms, wiped and sliced
2 red peppers, seeded, cored and diced
2 courgettes, chopped
8 oz/225g baby corn, chopped
4 oz/115g sunflower or pumpkin seeds, lightly toasted in a pan
1 tsp dried marjoram
1 tsp dried basil
4 oz/115g freshly grated Parmesan cheese
Salt and freshly ground black pepper

Preheat oven to gas mark 6, 200C/400F. Brush squash with oil and place flat side down on a baking sheet. Bake for 25-30 mins or until the flesh is beginning to soften. Leave to cool slightly. Melt the butter and add the garlic, mushrooms, peppers, baby corn, courgettes and herbs. Sauté together for a few minutes until the vegetables have softened but still retain some bite. Scoop out most of the flesh from the squash, being careful not to break the skin. Mix the flesh with the vegetables, season with salt and pepper, and add the seeds and about half the grated cheese.

Pile the filling into the squash skins, sprinkle with the remaining cheese and bake for a further 20-25 minutes until the filling is hot and the cheese browned.

Serves 4.

Root vegetable gratin

Humble root vegetables get a new lease of life, retaining their individual flavours, but soaking up the richness of the herbs, garlic and tomatoes as they're slowly baked. Serve it with a crisp green salad. It is also good as a side dish, alongside a savoury tart or filo pastry.

1 turnip, peeled, quartered and sliced ¼ inch thick
1 celeriac, peeled, quartered and sliced ¼ inch thick
2 large parsnips, peeled and sliced ¼ inch thick
4 potatoes, peeled and sliced ¼ inch thick
3 tomatoes, peeled and finely chopped
1 clove garlic, crushed
3 eggs, beaten
4 fl oz/100ml natural or Greek yogurt
4 fl oz/100ml single cream
1 tsp herbes de Provence
5 oz/140g Mozzarella cheese, thinly sliced
2 oz/55g freshly grated Parmesan cheese
Salt and freshly ground black pepper

Bring a large pan of lightly salted water to the boil, add the root vegetables and blanch for 3 minutes. Drain. Beat together the tomatoes, garlic, eggs, yogurt, cream and herbs, then season with salt and freshly ground black pepper.

To assemble the gratin, butter a large shallow baking dish. Cover the base with half the vegetables, pour over half the sauce and top with half the Mozzarella. Repeat, finishing with Mozzarella, and scatter over with Parmesan.

Bake in oven at gas mark 6, 200C/400F for 40-45 minutes until the vegetables are tender and the cheese is golden and bubbling. Serve hot.

Serves 4 or 6-8 as an accompaniment.

Baked polenta and mushroom gratin

Polenta is a staple part of the Italian diet, and is a basic mixture of cornmeal, water and salt, cooked until thick, and then served in a variety of ways. Here it's spread out like a slab, then sliced and baked in a simple tomato sauce, making a rustic dish with good flavours and textures. For some variation, it is also delicious baked in either the roasted red pepper sauce (see page 54), or the blue cheese and basil sauce (page 51).

For the polenta
   6 oz/170g polenta (cornmeal)
   1 pint/575ml water
   1 tsp salt

For the tomato sauce
   2 tbsp olive oil
   2 cloves garlic, crushed
   1 onion finely chopped
   8 fresh tomatoes, skinned and chopped or 14 oz/400g
     canned tomatoes, chopped
   4 tbsp fresh basil, finely chopped, or 2 tsp dried basil
   Salt and freshly ground black pepper

For the mushrooms
   2 oz/55g butter
   2 cloves garlic, crushed
   8 oz/225g chestnut mushrooms, sliced

For the topping
   4 oz/115g Gruyère cheese or Pecorino cheese, grated. If
   Pecorino isn't available, Parmesan can be used.

First make the polenta by bringing the water and salt to the boil. Gradually stir in the polenta, stirring constantly with a wooden spoon. Lower the heat and cook for 15-20 mins, stirring all the time. Add a little more water if it seems too thick. Turn onto a baking tray, spread out to approx. 1 in/2.5 cm thickness, and leave to cool.

   Next, heat the oil and sauté the garlic and onion until softened. Add the tomatoes and basil. Cover and simmer, stirring occasionally, for 25-30 mins. Season with salt and pepper.

Melt the butter and add the garlic and mushrooms and cook quickly for 2-3 mins. Butter a good sized baking dish. Slice the Polenta into squares about 3 ins/7.5cm across. To assemble the gratin, put a thin layer of tomato sauce over the base of the dish then scatter over half the mushrooms.

Arrange the polenta slices over this, then top with the remaining mushrooms and tomato sauce. Sprinkle with the grated cheese and bake at gas mark 6, 200C/400F for 30-35 mins until golden brown. Serve hot.

Serves 4-6.

Provençal gratin

This is a nice, simple, summer vegetable stew, made richer by baking with cheese and pine nuts. You could omit the topping, and serve it straight from the pan, but the finishing touch adds depth to both the flavour and fragrance of the dish.

3 tbsp olive oil
1 oz/30g butter
2 cloves garlic, crushed
1 onion peeled and thinly sliced
6 oz/170g green beans, topped, tailed and halved
2 peppers, 1 red and 1 yellow, cored, seeded and thickly
   sliced
2 courgettes, wiped and thickly sliced
8 oz/225g mushrooms, wiped and thickly sliced
1 tbsp fresh rosemary, finely chopped or 2 tsp dried
2 tsp dried oregano
4 fl oz/100ml dry red wine
14 oz/400g canned tomatoes, chopped
6 oz/170g Gruyère cheese, grated
4 oz/115g pine nuts (toasted in a pan until golden)
Salt and freshly ground black pepper

Heat oil and butter in a large, heavy based pan. Add the garlic and onion and sweat until translucent. Add the beans, peppers and courgettes, cover and cook gently until just softened.

Stir in herbs, mushrooms and wine, and continue to cook until the liquid has reduced slightly. Add the tomatoes with juice, half cover and simmer until stew is thick and most of the liquid has reduced.

Season. Butter a gratin or oven-proof dish, pile in the stew and scatter over the pine nuts and cheese. Bake in an oven gas mark 6, 200C/400F for 20-25 mins, until cheese is browned and bubbling. Serve hot.

Serves 4.

Gratin Dauphinoise

A popular French dish, this is a rich, creamy bake for thinly sliced potatoes, layered with leeks, garlic and Gruyère cheese. It's delicious in its own right as a main dish, served with a mixed salad and maybe some garlic bread, or would also be good as a way of serving potatoes as a side dish for a special meal.

**3lbs/1.35kg potatoes, washed and thinly sliced about
   ¼ inch thick
1 large leek, washed and thinly sliced
2 cloves garlic, crushed
3 oz/85g butter
12-16 fl oz/350-500ml double cream or use half single and
   half double
6 oz/170g Gruyère cheese, grated
Freshly ground nutmeg
Salt and freshly ground black pepper**

Using about 1 oz/30g of butter, grease a large oven-proof dish (use one you can serve from at the table). Layer half the potatoes, then season with half the garlic, some salt, pepper, and grated nutmeg (about ¼ tsp). Sprinkle with the sliced leek.

Cover with the remaining potatoes, and season again with garlic, salt and pepper. Top with the grated cheese. Pour the cream over the top, enough to generously cover the potatoes, and dot with the remaining 2 oz/55g of butter. Bake in oven at gas mark 5, 190C/375F for 1½-2 hours, or until the potatoes are tender and have absorbed most of the cream.

If the gratin appears too dry, add more cream during the cooking time. If browning too quickly, cover lightly with foil. Serve immediately.

Serves 4 or 6-8 as an accompaniment.

Fennel and mushroom gratin

Fennel is used a great deal in Mediterranean cooking, particularly in gratins of this style. It retains its firm texture and mild sweetness, being balanced by the tartness of the sauce and soft flesh of the mushrooms. Serve with something mild, such as creamed potatoes, or potato cake with chives, basil and goat's cheese (see page 43)

For the sauce
    2 onions, peeled and chopped
    3 cloves garlic, crushed
    3 tbsp olive oil
    1½ lb/675g ripe tomatoes, peeled and chopped
    1 tbsp tomato purée
    1 tbsp fresh rosemary, finely chopped or 2 tsp dried
    4 tbsp single cream

For the filling
    2 oz/55g butter
    3 fennel bulbs trimmed of base, woody outer leaves and stalks, thickly sliced
    8 oz/225g mushrooms, sliced
    1 tbsp lemon juice
    4 oz/115g freshly grated Parmesan cheese
    Salt and freshly ground black pepper

First make the sauce. Heat the oil in a pan and add the onions and two of the crushed garlic cloves. Cook gently until soft and translucent, then stir in the tomatoes, tomato purée and rosemary. Cook over a gentle heat, covered, until the sauce has thickened. Stir in the cream, season with salt and black pepper, and simmer for another few minutes. For the vegetables, melt the butter and add the remaining garlic. Add the sliced fennel and mushrooms and sauté, uncovered, for a few minutes until just beginning to soften. Add the lemon juice and cook until the liquid has reduced and the fennel is almost tender. Season, then pile into a buttered baking dish.

Pour over the sauce, mixing gently to combine with the vegetables, and sprinkle with the Parmesan. Bake for 20-30 minutes in oven gas mark 6, 200C/400F until the fennel is tender and the cheese is golden brown. Serve hot.

Serves 4.

Moussaka

Moussaka is a lovely dish — simple and rustic, with the flavours and scents reminiscent of its Greek origins. It is a fairly filling dish, so serve it with a light mixed salad, garnished with glistening black olives and chunks of salty white Feta cheese.

1 lb/450g aubergines, thinly sliced
1 lb/450g new potatoes
2 tbsp olive oil (plus a little extra for brushing)
3 cloves garlic, crushed
1 onion, finely chopped
8 oz/225g mushrooms, wiped and sliced
2 x 14 oz/400g canned tomatoes, chopped
1 tbsp tomato purée
4 fl oz/100ml red wine
1 tsp finely chopped fresh rosemary, or 1 tsp dried
1 tbsp finely chopped fresh basil, or 3 tsp dried
3 eggs
10 oz/285g natural yogurt
1 tbsp lemon juice
3 oz/85g freshly grated Parmesan cheese
8 sun-dried tomatoes, in oil, thinly sliced (optional)
Salt and freshly ground black pepper

Lay the aubergine slices in a colander, sprinkle with salt, and leave for 30 minutes to draw out the bitter juices. Rinse and pat dry. Blanch the potatoes in boiling water for 5 mins, drain and slice thinly. For the sauce, heat the oil in a large pan, add the garlic and onion and sauté until tender. Add the mushrooms, rosemary, tomatoes, tomato purée and red wine. Cover and cook gently for 15-20 mins. Season with salt and pepper and stir in the basil. Beat the eggs with the yogurt and lemon juice and season to taste.

To assemble the dish, brush a large, deep-sided baking dish with olive oil. Spread half the aubergine slices over the base of the dish, then half the potato slices, and pour over half of the tomato sauce. Top with the remaining aubergine, potato and tomato sauce. Pour over the egg mixture, scatter on the sun-dried tomatoes and sprinkle with the cheese. Bake in an oven gas mark 6, 200C/400F for 50 mins to 1 hour, until the vegetables are tender and the cheese is golden brown. Serve hot.
Serves 4-6.

PASTAS, GNOCCHI AND POLENTA

Spinach and Ricotta dumplings

Dumplings of this style, or gnocchi, are integral to Italian cuisine and are quick and simple to prepare. Once cooked, they are lovely baked in either a simple tomato sauce, or the roasted red pepper sauce (see page 54) topped with sliced Mozzarella and grated Parmesan. Alternatively, they can be drizzled with a little melted butter, sprinkled with Parmesan and browned under the grill.

1lb/450g fresh spinach, stemmed
8 oz/225g Ricotta cheese
2 oz/55g plain flour
1 egg, beaten
2 oz/55g freshly grated Parmesan cheese
Salt and freshly ground black pepper

Wash the spinach thoroughly, then pile into a large pot. Add a little water, and cook gently until wilted. Transfer to a colander and drain, squeezing out as much water from the spinach as you can. Chop finely. Combine the spinach with the Ricotta, and stir in the egg, flour, Parmesan and seasoning. Have ready a well-floured surface, then roll the mixture, about 1 tsp per dumpling, in the flour to form a ball.

Place the dumplings on a floured board. When ready to cook, bring a large pan of water to the boil, drop in the dumplings, about 5-6 at a time, and cook at a gentle boil for 3-4 mins until they rise to the surface. Remove with a slotted spoon and continue until all are cooked.

Serves 2-3.

Grilled polenta with coriander pesto

Pesto is traditionally made with basil, but coriander makes an interesting, spicier, variation. It goes well with the polenta, complementing its mild, slightly nutty flavour

For the pesto
   2 tbsp pumpkin seeds, lightly toasted in a pan
   6 tbsp fresh coriander, finely chopped
   3 tbsp flat leaf parsley, finely chopped
   1 clove garlic, crushed
   6 tbsp olive oil
   ½ tsp ground cumin
   1 oz/30g freshly grated Parmesan cheese
   1 tbsp fresh lime juice
   Salt and freshly ground black pepper

For the polenta
   8 oz/225g polenta (or cornmeal)
   1 oz/30g butter
   2 tbsp olive oil
   Salt and freshly ground black pepper

Place all the ingredients for the pesto in a blender or food processor and blend until puréed and fairly smooth. Transfer to a bowl, cover and refrigerate.

To make the polenta, bring 1¼ pints/700ml salted water to the boil and gradually pour in the polenta, stirring all the time. Lower the heat and continue to cook, stirring, for 15-20 mins until thick.

Stir in the butter, season, and spoon into a greased, shallow baking tray spreading out until flat. When cool, cut into slices and brush each side with olive oil. Place under a hot grill and cook for 3-5 mins on each side until lightly browned. Serve each slice spread with pesto.

Serves 4-8.

Tagliatelle with grilled peppers, courgettes and herbs

The soft flesh of the grilled vegetables contrasts nicely with the bite of the pasta, their flavour adding smokiness and a rich texture to the dish. Again, fresh pasta gives a more delicate end result, but if you haven't got any, use dried pasta.

12 oz/350g fresh or dried tagliatelle
2 oz/55g butter
2 cloves of garlic, crushed
3 tomatoes, skinned and chopped
4 peppers (2 red, 2 yellow), halved lengthways, cored and seeded
2 courgettes, sliced in half lengthways
2 tbsp fresh herbs, finely chopped or 1 tbsp dried — choose from rosemary, basil, sage, thyme, or chervil
4 tbsp Greek yogurt or crème fraiche
4 oz/115g freshly grated Parmesan cheese
Olive oil
Salt and freshly ground black pepper

Brush the courgettes and peppers with olive oil. Place under a hot grill until the skins are browning and the flesh is softened. The courgettes will cook quicker, so remove them first and continue to grill the peppers until the skin is almost blackened. Place the peppers in a bowl, cover and set aside.

When cool enough to handle, chop the courgettes into large chunks. Skin the peppers and slice into thin shreds. Have a pan ready of boiling salted water for the pasta, with a few drops of olive oil added.

Melt the butter in a pan and add the garlic and chopped tomatoes. Cook gently until the tomatoes are pulpy, then add the courgettes, peppers and herbs and keep warm over a gentle heat. Cook the pasta until just tender but still with some bite (about 6-8 minutes for fresh, 8-10 minutes for dried). Just before the pasta is ready, add the yogurt or crème fraiche to the vegetables. Heat gently and season with black pepper.

Drain the pasta in a colander and add to the vegetables, tossing gently to mix everything together. Serve in warm bowls, sprinkled with the Parmesan.

Serves 4.

Tagliatelle with green beans, Feta and pesto

The flavours and textures of this pasta dish are varied and interesting — the green beans add bite, the Feta adds a mild saltiness, and the rocket lends the dish a nutty flavour. The cream adds richness to the dish, so serve it with something clean and light, such as a mixed green salad and a side dish of thinly-sliced plum tomatoes.

12 oz/350g fresh or dried tagliatelle
2 tbsp olive oil
2 cloves garlic, crushed
8 oz/225g green beans, topped and tailed
2 large fresh tomatoes, skinned and chopped
2 tbsp pesto
5 fl oz/150 ml crème fraiche or fresh cream
6 oz/170g Feta cheese, crumbled
3 oz/85g rocket salad leaves, torn into shreds
1 oz/30g pine nuts, lightly-toasted in a pan
1 tbsp chopped fresh basil
3 oz/85g freshly grated Parmesan cheese
Salt and freshly ground black pepper

First make the sauce. Heat the olive oil in a pan and add the garlic. Sauté gently for a minute then stir in the green beans. Add the tomatoes, cover and cook gently for five minutes. Stir in the pesto and crème fraiche or cream and cook until the sauce is slightly thickened. Season with pepper. Cook the pasta in plenty of boiling salted water until just tender but still with bite — about 6-8 minutes for fresh pasta, 8-10 minutes for dried. Drain well, toss with the sauce and stir in the Feta cheese and rocket. Serve immediately, in warm bowls, sprinkled with the pine nuts, basil and Parmesan.
Serves 4.

Pasta with stewed peppers and cherry tomatoes

This is a summery pasta dish that's quick and simple to prepare, with colours which are bright and flavours that are vibrant. It's best made with one of the many varieties of ready-made fresh pastas such as ravioli filled with either cheeses, mushrooms or spinach.

11 oz/325g fresh pasta
2 tbsp olive oil
1 oz/30g butter
2 cloves garlic, crushed
1 red and 1 yellow pepper, cored, seeded and thinly sliced
10 oz/285g cherry tomatoes, stems removed
2 tbsp fresh basil, finely chopped or 3 tsp dried
4 oz/115g freshly grated Parmesan cheese
Salt and freshly ground black pepper

Heat together the oil and butter in a heavy based pan. Add the garlic and peppers, cover and stew gently, stirring occasionally until the peppers are tender, about 15-20 mins. Have ready a large pan of boiling salted water. Add a few drops of oil to the water and cook the pasta for 6-8 mins until just tender but still with some bite. Just before the pasta is ready, stir the basil and tomatoes into the peppers and cook quickly over a medium heat to allow the tomatoes to warm but not overcook.

Drain the pasta, add to the peppers and toss everything together. Season and serve immediately, sprinkled with Parmesan cheese.

Serves 3-4.

Pumpkin gnocchi baked in tomato and basil sauce

This is a traditional Italian dish of golden dumplings baked in a creamy tomato sauce. If pumpkin isn't available, butternut squash can be used. Both will give the gnocchi a good flavour and colour.

For the gnocchi
 1 lb/450g peeled and seeded pumpkin, cubed
 8 oz/225g potatoes, unpeeled
 4 oz/115g plain flour
 1 egg, beaten
 2 oz/55g grated Parmesan cheese
 ¼ tsp ground nutmeg
 Salt and freshly ground black pepper

For the sauce
 2 tbsp olive oil
 1 onion, chopped
 3 cloves of garlic, crushed
 1 lb/450g tomatoes, skinned and chopped
   or 1 x 14 oz/400g canned tomatoes, chopped
 2 tbsp red wine
 4 fl oz/100ml single cream
 2 tbsp chopped fresh basil
 Salt and freshly ground black pepper

For the topping
 2 oz/55g freshly grated Parmesan cheese

First make the gnocchi. Bring a pan of salted water to the boil, add the potatoes and cook for 5 minutes. Add the pumpkin and cook for a further 10-15 mins until both vegetables are tender. Drain in a colander, and remove the skins from the potatoes. Mash potatoes in a bowl, add the remaining ingredients, combine well, cover and refrigerate for at least half an hour.

   For the sauce, heat the oil and add the onion and garlic. Sauté until tender then stir in the tomatoes and wine. Cover and simmer for 15 mins, then stir in the cream, basil, and seasoning. Simmer gently for a further 5 mins until the sauce has thickened.

To shape the gnocchi, drop by teaspoons on to a well floured surface and roll gently into the flour to form balls. Place on a floured board. Bring a pan of water to the boil, reduce heat to a gentle boil, and add the gnocchi, about 5-6 at a time. Poach for 4-5 mins, keeping the water at a gentle boil, until the gnocchi rise to the surface. Remove and transfer to a large baking dish, arranging the gnocchi in a single layer. Continue until all the gnocchi are cooked, pour over the sauce and sprinkle with the Parmesan. Bake in the oven gas mark 6, 200C/400F for 30 mins until the cheese is lightly browned and the sauce is bubbling.

Serves 4.

Spinach and three cheese lasagne

If you can get hold of fresh sheets of lasagne, or are good at making your own pasta, most definitely use that, since the flavour and texture are infinitely better. However, the 'no pre-cook' variety is also good and works well in this dish.

For the filling
    About 10-12 sheets fresh or 'no pre-cook' lasagne
    2 lb/900g fresh spinach, washed, stemmed and chopped
    3 peppers, one of each (red, yellow and orange)
    2 tbsp olive oil, plus extra for brushing
    3 cloves garlic, crushed
    1 onion, finely chopped
    ½ tbsp fresh rosemary, or 2 tbsp dried
    4 oz/115g Mozzarella cheese
    8 oz/225g Ricotta cheese
    4 oz/115g freshly grated Parmesan cheese

For the sauce
    1 oz/30g butter
    1 oz/30g plain flour
    ¾ pint/450ml milk
    Grating of fresh nutmeg
    Salt and freshly ground black pepper

Halve peppers lengthways, core and seed, brush with oil, place under a hot grill until blistered and blackened. Transfer to a bowl and cover. Heat oil and sauté garlic and onion until softened. Stir in the rosemary and add the spinach in batches, cooking until just wilted. Remove from heat and mix in the Ricotta and Parmesan cheese. Season. Peel the skins from the peppers. Slice thickly and mix with spinach.

Melt the butter, stir in the flour and cook for a minute. Gradually stir in the milk and cook until smooth and thick, stirring constantly. Season with salt, pepper and nutmeg.

Heat oven to gas mark 6, 200C/400F. Butter a large, shallow baking dish. Spread a layer of spinach over the base, cover with half the lasagne, then half the Mozzarella and half the sauce. Repeat, finishing with the sauce. Bake for 30-35 minutes, until bubbling and golden brown.

Serves 4-6.

SAVOURY TARTS AND PASTRY DISHES

Gougère

This French-style choux pastry is enriched by the cheese and herbs, making a puffed, golden pastry case which can then be filled in a variety of ways. Try Peperonata (see page 103), Succotash (page 93), or a filling of freshly cooked spinach, mixed with a little cream and some crumbly goat's cheese.

2 oz/55g butter
5 fl oz/150ml water
2½ oz/75g plain flour
2 eggs, beaten
3 oz/85g grated Cheddar or Gruyère cheese
½ tsp herbes de Provence
Salt and freshly ground black pepper

Place the water and butter in a pan and heat gently until the butter has melted. Bring to the boil, then remove from heat and quickly tip in the flour, beating well with a wooden spoon. Mix to a smooth paste. Beat in the eggs, a little at a time, until the mixture is smooth and glossy. Beat in 2 oz/55g of the cheese, the herbs and season with salt and pepper. Heat oven to gas mark 6, 200C/400F. Grease a baking tray and sprinkle lightly with cold water. Create a ring of dollops of the pastry mix, a tablespoonful for each one, but do not flatten these. Place another tablespoonful in the middle of the circle and flatten this out with the back of the spoon to make a base. Sprinkle with the remaining cheese and bake for 35-40 minutes, until golden and puffy. Serve hot from the oven.
Serves 2-3.

Leek, Feta and walnut parcels

Individual pastries make an impressive dish for a main meal, served perhaps in a sauce, or surrounded by a selection of colourful mixed lettuce leaves. These parcels have a filling aromatic with herbs, garlic, and gently stewed leeks. If Feta isn't available, you could use a crumbly goat's cheese instead.

½ package filo pastry (8oz/225g). (See page 11)
4 leeks, trimmed and thinly sliced
8 oz/225g Feta cheese
4 oz/115g walnuts, roasted in hot oven for five minutes and finely chopped.
6 oz/170g butter
1 clove garlic, crushed
2 tsp coarse grain mustard
1 tbsp fresh herbs or ½ tbsp dried — use sage, chervil or marjoram
Salt and freshly ground black pepper

Melt 2 oz/55g butter in a large pan and add the garlic, leeks and herbs. Cook gently for about 10 minutes until the leeks are softened. Remove from heat and drain off any excess liquid. Add the walnuts and mustard to the leeks, crumble in the cheese and mix well. Season with pepper. Unfold the filo pastry. If the sheets are large, slice them in half widthways.

Keep the sheets covered with a damp cloth. Melt the remaining 4 oz/115g of butter. To make four individual parcels, spread one filo sheet out on a board and brush with melted butter. This sheet will be the base of one parcel. Continue layering the pastry in this way, using about 4-5 sheets per parcel. Repeat until you've layered four piles of pastry sheets. Divide the filling between each pile of sheets and fold up the sides and ends to enclose the filling.

Place with the fold side down on a buttered baking sheet and brush the tops with melted butter. Bake in the oven gas mark 6, 200C/400F for 30-35 minutes or until browned and crisp.
Serves 4.

Onion tart

This is a typically French tart with a simple filling of onions, stewed until meltingly tender, which contrasts well with the buttery, crisp pastry. Serve it hot or warm, with a colourful mixed salad and some lightly cooked green beans.

8 oz/225g shortcrust pastry
1½ lbs/675g onions, weighed after peeling, thinly sliced
2 oz/55g butter
3 cloves garlic, crushed
1 tsp salt
2 whole eggs
1 egg yolk
4 fl oz/100ml cream
1 tsp herbes de Provence
1 tsp Dijon mustard
Freshly ground black pepper

Roll out the pastry and line a greased 9in/23cm loose-bottomed tart tin (see page 12). Partially bake in oven at gas mark 6, 200C/400F for 15 minutes and set aside.

For the filling, melt the butter in a large, heavy based pan. Add the garlic, onions and salt. Cover and stew gently for 15-20 minutes until the onions are very tender, stirring occasionally.

Beat the eggs with the cream, herbs and mustard. Season with pepper and stir in the onions. Pour into the crust and bake in the oven gas mark 6, 200C/400F for 35-40 minutes until the filling is set and lightly browned. Makes one 9in/23cm tart.

Serves 4-6.

Three cheese parcels

These are a wonderful combination of crisp, golden pastry, with a filling of cheeses that is soft, creamy and aromatic. They are as much of a pleasure to make as they are to eat, their taste belying their simplicity.

2 onions, peeled and finely chopped
2 cloves of garlic, crushed
2 tbsp olive oil
½ tbsp fresh rosemary, finley chopped
2 tbsp fresh basil, finely chopped
8 oz/225g Ricotta cheese
4 oz/115g crumbly blue cheese (use Roquefort
or Danish Blue)
4 oz/115g freshly grated Parmesan cheese
3-4oz/85-115g butter, melted
16 large sheets of filo pastry
Salt and freshly ground black pepper

Heat the oil and fry the onions with the garlic until soft and translucent. Stir in the rosemary, season and set aside. Cream together the three cheeses in a bowl, mix in the basil, season, stir in the onion mixture and set aside.

Melt the butter and lay out one sheet of filo pastry, keeping the other sheets covered with a damp cloth. Brush the pastry with melted butter, top with another sheet and brush again with butter. Continue in this way until you have layered four sheets. Repeat with the remaining sheets, layering four sheets at a time to make four piles.

Divide the cheese mixture between the four piles, spooning into the centre then folding up the sides of the sheets to create a sealed parcel. Place seam side down on a baking tray, and brush with melted butter. Bake in oven gas mark 6, 200C/ 400F for 15-20 minutes until crisp and golden. Serve immediately. Makes four parcels.

Serves 4.

Coulibiac

Coulibiac is a Russian speciality, traditionally made with a Brioche dough and including fish in the filling. Life is made easier by using ready-made puff pastry, and the filling here includes layers of spinach, mushrooms, tomatoes and Mozzarella, making it both colourful and attractive. This makes an impressive dish for a dinner party, and is useful on such an occasion since all the preparation can be done in advance, leaving only the baking of the dish to be done at the time.

1 onion, peeled and chopped
1 clove garlic, crushed
1 tbsp olive oil
6 oz/170g brown rice
12 fl oz/350ml vegetable stock
2 tsp herbes de Provence, or 1 tsp dried basil and 1 tsp
   dried rosemary
1 oz/30g butter
8 oz/225g mushrooms, sliced
1 lb/450g fresh spinach, washed and stemmed or 8oz/
   225g frozen spinach, thawed and chopped
2 red peppers, grilled, skinned and sliced (see page 11)
14 oz/400g canned tomatoes, drained and sliced.
8 oz/225g Mozzarella cheese, sliced
2 eggs, hard boiled and sliced
14 oz/400g puff pastry
1 egg beaten
Salt and freshly ground black pepper

Sesame seeds or poppy seeds for garnish

Heat oil in a large pan and sauté onion and garlic for a couple of minutes. Add rice, herbs, and stock. Bring to the boil, reduce heat and simmer, covered, until rice is cooked and has absorbed the liquid. Leave to cool. Melt the butter and add the mushrooms, cooking over a fairly high heat until softened. Stir in the rice. Cook the spinach in a small amount of boiling water until wilted. Drain in a colander and squeeze out excess water. Chop finely and season with salt and pepper.

Roll out pastry to a rectangle, about 12x14 ins/30x35cm. Grease a flat baking sheet and lay pastry on this. Leaving a large border to fold up sides and edges, begin to layer ingredients onto the pastry. Start with a third of the spinach, add a third of the rice, then a layer of tomatoes, slices of peppers, Mozzarella cheese, and repeat until all the ingredients are layered, finishing with cheese and egg slices. Fold up sides and edges to securely enclose the filling. Brush with beaten egg and sprinkle with sesame or poppy seeds. Bake at gas mark 5, 190C/375F for 30-40 minutes until golden brown. Carefully remove from the baking sheet onto a serving dish, and serve hot, cut into thick slices, with the roasted red pepper sauce (see page 54).

Serves 4-6.

CAFE ALBA, OTAGO STREET — Situated in the West End, this cafe has a casual atmosphere, with a wide choice of inexpensive, home-made vegetarian dishes.

Spinach and pine nut tart

I frequently get requests to make this tart for parties and family gatherings, as it is not only delicious, but also very attractive with a dense, green filling, speckled with golden pine nuts. Serve it hot or warm, alongside the tomato and Mozzarella salad (see page 34), which complements the colours and flavours beautifully.

8 oz/225g shortcrust pastry
2 lbs/900g fresh or 1 lb/450g frozen spinach
1 small leek
2 oz/55g butter
1 clove garlic, crushed
1 tbsp fresh basil, chopped or 1 tsp dried
2 whole eggs
1 egg yolk
6 fl oz/175ml double cream
4 oz/115g freshly grated Parmesan cheese
3 tbsp pine nuts, lightly toasted in a pan until golden
Salt and freshly ground black pepper

Line a 9in/23cm loose-bottomed flan tin with the pastry and leave to rest in a fridge for half an hour. Prick the base and bake at gas mark 6, 200C/400F for 15 minutes. Melt butter in a large pan and add garlic, leek and basil.

Cook over a medium heat for a few minutes. Add the spinach in handfuls at a time and cook until it has just wilted. When all the spinach has been added and cooked, drain the mixture in a colander to remove excess liquid. Beat together the eggs, egg yolk and cream.

Add the Parmesan cheese and season with salt and pepper. Mix in the spinach and pour into the pastry case. Scatter the pine nuts over the tart. Bake at gas mark 6, 200C/400F for 30-35 minutes until lightly set and golden brown. Makes one 9in/23cm tart.

Serves 4-6.

Pissaladière

Ready-made puff pastry makes a delicious thin and crispy crust for this Provençal onion pizza, and also makes it quick and easy to put together. Traditionally, pissaladière is garnished with anchovies, but I've omitted them and added Parmesan cheese instead, which bakes to a delicious, golden topping.

1 lb/450g puff pastry
4 lbs/1.8kg onions, peeled and thinly sliced
2 cloves garlic, crushed
3 tbsp olive oil
2 oz/55g butter
3-4 tbsp red wine
1 tbsp fresh rosemary, finely chopped or 2 tsp dried
8 oz/225g Feta cheese, crumbled
5 oz/140g green or black olives, pitted and halved
4 oz/115g freshly grated Parmesan cheese
Salt and freshly ground black pepper

Heat the oil and butter in a large, non-stick pan. Add the garlic and onions and cook gently until translucent. Stir in the wine and rosemary, cover and cook gently, stirring occasionally, for 30-45 minutes until onions are soft and almost caramelised. If the onions are sticking to the pan add a little water (or a spot more wine) during the cooking time.

Remove from heat, mix in the crumbled Feta cheese and season with salt and pepper. Preheat oven to gas mark 7, 220C/ 425F. Lightly oil a large shallow-sided baking dish. Roll out pastry and line dish, allowing pastry to cover base and sides. Spread onion mixture over pastry, dot with olives and sprinkle with the Parmesan cheese. Bake for 20-25 minutes until crust is browned and cheese golden. Serve hot or warm.

Serves 6.

Aubergine tart

Layers of aubergine, rich and smoky in flavour, are baked in a custard fragrant with Parmesan cheese and basil. Serve this attractive tart with something simple — a tomato salad and buttered new potatoes, or some freshly cooked pasta tossed in fruity olive oil and chopped rosemary.

8 oz/225g shortcrust pastry
3 good sized aubergines, sliced ¼ inch thick
1 red pepper
Olive oil for brushing
2 whole eggs
1 egg yolk
6 fl oz/175ml double cream
2 oz/55g freshly grated Parmesan cheese
2 tbsp fresh basil, finely chopped or 3 tsp dried basil
Salt and freshly ground black pepper

Roll out pastry to line a 9in/23cm base tart tin (see page 12). Partially bake and set aside. Place aubergine slices and pepper on a baking tray and brush with olive oil, turning to coat in oil.

Bake at gas mark 6, 200C/400F until aubergine slices are tender and lightly browned, about 5-10 minutes each side, and the skin of the pepper is blistered. The pepper will take longer — up to 40 minutes — to roast. When the aubergine slices are ready, remove from heat onto a plate. When the pepper is ready, transfer to a bowl, cover and set aside. When it's cool enough to handle, remove skin, core and seeds, and slice the pepper into strips.

Beat together the eggs, egg yolk, cream, Parmesan cheese and basil. Season. Layer the aubergine slices on the pastry case and pour the custard over the top. Place pepper slices on the surface. Bake in oven gas mark 6, 200C/400F for 30-40 mins, until golden brown. Allow to cool for 5-10 mins before serving. Makes one 9in/23cm tart.

Serves 4-6.

Trio of vegetables wrapped in filo

Layers of crisp, golden filo enclose a filling of spinach, cheeses and roasted vegetables. This is a handsome dish, good to serve for a special occasion or dinner party. The french goat's cheese is now available at many major supermarkets, or good delicatessens. Try to use the type that comes cut from a log (remove the rind). However, if you can't get hold of it many British goat's cheeses are now widely available.

1 large aubergine, trimmed and sliced ¼ inch thick
1 red and yellow pepper, halved lengthways, cored and
   seeded
Olive oil for brushing
2 lbs/900g fresh spinach, washed, stemmed and chopped
2 cloves garlic, crushed
2 oz/55g butter
1 tsp basil
8 oz/225g Ricotta cheese
8 oz/225g French goat's cheese, crumbled
2 eggs beaten
12 large sheets of filo pastry, approx 8 oz/225g
4 oz/115g butter, melted
2 oz/55g walnuts, chopped
Salt and freshly ground black pepper

Preheat oven to gas mark 6, 200C/400F. Brush peppers and aubergine slices with oil, place on tray and roast in oven. Give aubergines ten minutes on each side, and the peppers 25-30 minutes, or until the skins are blistered.

Place peppers in a bowl, cover and set aside. Heat butter in a large pan, add the garlic and sauté for a minute, Add the spinach, cooking quickly until wilted.

Remove from heat and drain off excess liquid. Beat together the cheeses and eggs, season, add basil and stir in the spinach. Remove pepper skins and slice the peppers and aubergine into strips. Brush a large, shallow-sided baking tray with melted butter. Lay one filo sheet on the tray, allowing it to cover the base and hang over the sides of the tray. Brush the pastry with melted butter, then continue to layer the filo sheets, brushing each sheet with butter, until all the sheets have been used. Scatter half the walnuts over pastry, spoon over half the spinach, leaving enough pastry clear at the sides and ends to fold over into a parcel.

Lay the pepper and aubergine strips over the filling, and cover with the remaining spinach mixture. Scatter over the remaining walnuts, and carefully fold up the ends and then the sides of the pastry to enclose the filling.

Carefully turn it over so that the seam side is on the base of the tray. Brush with melted butter, and bake at gas mark 6, 200C/400F for 40-50 minutes until crisp and golden brown. Serve hot.

Serves 6.

Leek and Lanark Blue tart

Lanark Blue is a strongly flavoured, slightly salty, blue cheese made from ewe's milk. Produced in Lanarkshire, it is a fairly recent addition to the wealth of Scottish cheeses. The sharp flavour combines well with the slight sweetness of the leeks, while the semi-hard texture adds a gentle creaminess. If it's not available, Roquefort would make the best alternative, or failing that, Stilton or Gorgonzola could be used. All are cheeses with strong flavours and crumbly textures, which work well in this dish.

8 oz/225g shortcrust pastry
4 medium sized leeks, trimmed and sliced into thin rounds
3 oz/85g butter
2 cloves garlic, crushed
2 eggs
4 fl oz/100ml double cream
2 tsp coarse grain mustard
4 oz/115g Lanark Blue (or alternative cheese), crumbled
Salt and freshly ground black pepper

Grease a 9 ins/23cm loose-bottomed flan tin. Roll out the pastry, line the tin and partially bake in an oven at gas mark mark 6, 200C/400F for 15 minutes.

To make the filling, melt the butter in a large pan, add the garlic and leeks, cover and cook gently for 10-15 minutes until the leeks are tender. Beat together the eggs and cream, stir in the mustard, cheese and leeks, and season with salt and freshly ground black pepper. Pour into the partially baked crust and bake at the same temperature for 30-40 minutes until the filling is set and golden brown. Serve hot or warm. Makes one 9in/23cm tart.

Serves 4-6.

STOVE-TOP STEWS

Succotash

I tried this after seeing Sophie Grigson cook corn in this way on television and I have become a complete convert. Corn on the cob has the nice, but tiresome, habit of usually being served up boiled and coated with butter. Here, the kernels are scraped off, keeping all the flavour, and are stewed with beans, cream and coriander. The result is a dish loaded with flavour and warm spiciness, which goes well with the cornmeal and Gruyère pancakes, served hot from the pan (see page 107).

**4 fresh heads of sweetcorn, trimmed of leaves and fibres
1 red pepper, cored seeded and diced
8 spring onions, trimmed and chopped
2 oz/55g butter
14 oz/400g canned borlotti beans, drained and rinsed
5 fl oz/150ml single cream
1 tbsp freshly squeezed lemon juice
2 tbsp finely chopped fresh coriander
Salt and freshly ground black pepper**

Holding the corn in a large pan, scrape off the kernels. Scrape the cob to extract any milky liquid, adding this to the pan. Mix in the spring onions, diced pepper and butter. Add a little water, about ¼ pint/150ml, cover and cook over a medium heat for about 10-15 mins, until the corn is almost tender. Add the beans, cream, lemon juice and coriander. Season, cover and continue to cook for a further 5-10 mins, until the vegetables are tender and the dish has slightly thickened. Serve hot.
    Serves 2-3.

Pinto bean and vegetable korma

Pinto beans are small beans with a buttery texture and rich flavour. Their dark brown colour, combined with the orange and yellow tones of the vegetables, makes this a colourful stew with a rich aroma and flavour. Serve with fragrant pilau rice and hot chapatis or naan bread.

1 large sweet potato, diced into good-sized pieces
1 large or 2 small, butternut squash, peeled, seeded and diced into good sized pieces
Corn kernels scraped from two heads of sweetcorn
8 oz/225g mushrooms, wiped and quartered
1 lb/450g tomatoes, skinned and chopped, or 14oz/400g canned tomatoes, chopped
½ tsp fennel seeds
½ tsp cumin seeds
2 tbsp sesame seeds
2 tbsp olive oil
1 onion, peeled and finely chopped
3 cloves garlic, crushed
2 fresh chillis, seeded and finely chopped
2 tsp ground coriander
1 tsp ground cumin
1 oz/30g creamed coconut, dissolved in a ¼ pint/150ml of boiling water
14 oz/400g canned pinto beans, drained and rinsed
4 fl oz/100ml cream

3 tbsp finely chopped fresh coriander to garnish

Lightly toast the fennel, cumin and sesame seeds in a pan. Heat the oil in a large pan and add the garlic and onion. Sauté for a couple of minutes, then add the remaining spices. Cook gently for a minute, then add the toasted seeds, vegetables, tomatoes and coconut water. Cover and cook gently for 15 mins, adding a little more water if it seems too dry. Stir in the pinto beans and continue to cook gently for a further 5-10 minutes. Stir in the cream and fresh coriander, partially cover and simmer for 5-10 minutes until the stew is rich and thick and vegetables tender. Serve immediately, garnished with fresh coriander leaves.
Serves 4-6.

Grilled aubergine caponata

Grilling aubergines gives them a lovely smoky flavour, which adds depth to this Sicilian-style dish. The flavours are piquant, verging on sweet and sour. Serve this with some noodles, or crusty Italian bread.

- 1 large aubergine, sliced ¼ inch thick
- 4 tbsp olive oil, plus extra for brushing
- 1 onion, peeled and chopped
- 1 clove garlic, crushed
- 6 fresh tomatoes skinned and chopped or 14 oz/400g canned tomatoes
- 4 oz/115g mushrooms, wiped and sliced
- 1 tsp paprika
- ½ tsp cayenne pepper
- 1½ tsp red wine vinegar
- 10 black olives, pitted and chopped
- 2 tbsp fresh basil or parsley, finely chopped
- Salt and freshly ground black pepper

Brush the aubergine slices liberally with oil and place under a hot grill. Cook for 3-5 mins on each side until they are lightly browned and tender. Remove from heat and chop into large chunks. Heat 4 tbsp of olive oil in a large pan and add onion and garlic. Sauté until tender then add the tomatoes, mushrooms, spices and cook gently, covered, for 10-15 mins. Add the sugar and vinegar and simmer, uncovered, for a further 5-10 mins until rich and thick. Stir in the aubergines, olives and basil or parsley, season to taste. Serve hot or warm.

Serves 2.

Pumpkin and chick-pea stew

A mildly spiced stew with warming colours and flavours which is a good one to make in the autumn when bulbous orange and yellow pumpkins are filling the shelves in time for Hallow-een. Pumpkin flesh cooks to a soft texture, and has a mildly nutty flavour, which contrasts nicely with the bite of the chick-peas. Serve this with hot cornbread (see page 109) to com-plement the flavours.

14 oz/400g canned chick-peas, drained and rinsed
2 tbsp olive oil
2 oz/55g butter
1 clove garlic, crushed
1 onion, peeled and chopped
1 tsp ground cumin
1 tsp ground coriander
1 tsp fennel seeds
1 tsp dried basil or oregano
½ tsp chilli powder
14 oz /400g canned tomatoes chopped
2 lbs/900g pumpkin, peeled, seeded and diced into good
**   sized pieces**
8 oz/225g chestnut mushrooms, wiped and sliced
¼ pint/150ml vegetable stock
2 tbsp fresh coriander, finely chopped
Salt and freshly ground black pepper

Natural yogurt to serve

Melt the butter with the oil in a large pan and add the garlic and onion. Sauté until the onion has softened, then add the spices and herbs and cook for a couple of minutes longer. Add the pumpkin, mushrooms, tomatoes and vegetable stock. Cover and simmer for about 20-25 mins, or until the pumpkin is almost tender, stirring occasionally and adding a little more stock if necessary to prevent it from drying out. Add the chick-peas and fresh coriander and simmer until the pumpkin is ten-der. Season and serve in warmed bowls, topped with a swirl of yogurt.
Serves 4-6.

Mushroom risotto

Porcini are dried wild mushrooms, and are available from good quality delicatessens. They're expensive, but just a tiny amount adds a wonderful. rich, earthy mushroom flavour. A good risotto needs the proper rice, so use the Italian Arborio rice, to achieve an authentic, creamy result. It is available from Italian grocers, and some major supermarkets.

1 oz/30g dried porcini mushrooms
1 pint/575ml vegetable stock
2 oz/55g butter
2 cloves garlic, crushed
1 onion, peeled and finely chopped
½ tbsp fresh thyme, finely chopped or 1 tsp of dried
½ tbsp fresh rosemary, finely chopped or 1 tsp dried
8 oz/225g mushrooms, wiped and sliced
8 oz/225g Arborio rice
4 fl oz/100ml marsala wine or dry white wine
4 oz/115g freshly grated Parmesan cheese
Salt and freshly ground black pepper

Pour enough boiling water over the porcini to cover, and leave to soak for 30 minutes. Drain, reserving the liquid and chop the porcini. Combine the soaking liquid with the stock in a pan and bring to a simmer. Melt the butter in a large heavy based pan, add the garlic and onion and sweat until translucent. Stir in herbs, porcini and mushrooms, and sauté for a few minutes. Add the rice and stir to coat the grains. Add the wine and a ladleful of stock. Simmer gently until the liquid is absorbed. Add another couple of ladlefuls of stock, just enough to wet the rice, cover and continue to cook until absorbed, stirring occasionally.

Repeat in this way, adding only a ladleful or two of stock at a time, until the rice is tender and the risotto is rich and creamy. This should take about 30 minutes. Season with lots of black pepper, some salt, and stir in the Parmesan. Serve immediately. Serves 3-4.

Couscous

The word couscous is used to describe the whole dish — a spicy vegetable casserole, and the grain itself. It is an Algerian dish, and French Algerians now operate a number of couscous houses in Paris, where it's served in the traditional way — a bowl of couscous, a bowl of casserole, a bowl of chick-pea stew, and a bowl of spicy sauce. This is a simplified version, incorporating the spices and chick-peas into the casserole.

4 oz/115g butter
1 tbsp olive oil
2 cloves garlic, crushed
2 large onions, peeled and chopped
2 tsp ground cumin
2 tsp ground coriander
1 tsp paprika
1 tsp chilli powder
14 oz/400g canned tomatoes, chopped
3 large carrots, scrubbed and thickly sliced
1 cauliflower, trimmed and cut into florets
1 lb/450g butternut squash or turnip
4 large potatoes, scrubbed and cubed
1 aubergine, cubed
4 large courgettes, thickly sliced
14 oz/400g canned chick-peas, drained and rinsed
1-1½ pints/575-850ml vegetable stock
1 lb/450g couscous, available from supermarkets or Indian stores
1 large bunch of fresh coriander, finely chopped
Salt and freshly ground black pepper

Melt 2 oz/55g butter and the olive oil in a large pan. Add the garlic and onion. Sauté gently until tender then stir in the spices (but not the fresh coriander). Cook for a minute then add the tomatoes, vegetables, chick-peas and 1 pint/575ml of the stock. Simmer until the vegetables are tender, adding more stock as necessary to keep quite a lot of liquid in the casserole. When cooked, add the fresh coriander and season with salt and freshly ground black pepper. For the couscous, put the grain in a large bowl and pour in just enough water to cover it (about 1-1½pints/575-850ml). Set aside until the water is absorbed then rub the grain between your fingers to separate it and rub in the other 2 oz/55g butter, making sure there are no lumps. When ready to serve, heat the couscous in a sieve over the casserole, or covered in a tray in the oven. Serve the grain and casserole in large bowls, so everyone can help themselves.

Serves 6.

Stir-fry with lime and coriander

This basic stir-fry sauce is vamped up with fresh lime and coriander, resulting in a fragrant dish with a hint of citrus. Serve alongside egg noodles or on a bed of fluffy rice.

2 large courgettes, sliced into rounds ¼ inch thick
1 red pepper, cored, seeded and thinly sliced
6 oz/170g mushrooms, wiped and sliced
4 oz/115g baby corn, halved
4 oz/115g mange tout, topped and tailed
Juice of one lime, freshly squeezed, and grated zest
**   of ½ lime**
1 tbsp dry sherry
1 tbsp peeled and grated fresh root ginger
3 tbsp soy sauce
1 tbsp caster sugar
2 cloves garlic, crushed
2 tbsp sunflower oil or toasted sesame oil
A large bunch of finely chopped fresh coriander
Salt and freshly ground black pepper

Have all the vegetables prepared before you begin to cook. For the sauce, combine the lime juice, zest, sugar, sherry, soy sauce and ginger in a bowl. Heat the oil in a wok or heavy-based frying pan. Add the garlic and vegetables, keeping the heat quite high. Stir-fry for about 5 mins, until just softening but still fairly crisp. Pour in the sauce, mix well and continue to stir-fry until the vegetables are just tender and glazed with the sauce. Stir in the coriander, season to taste, and serve immediately.
    Serves 4.

Chilli with red and black beans

This is an old favourite, but it makes a good spicy stew that's easy to put together, with a nice mix of colours and flavours. Be careful to wash your hands after handling the fresh chilli, as they're powerful and cause a burning sensation. Serve this in bowls, topped with yogurt, with slices of hot, fresh, cornmeal and sun-dried tomato bread (see page 114).

2 tbsp olive oil
1 onion, peeled and chopped
2 cloves garlic, crushed
1 fresh chilli, seeded and finely chopped
2 tsp ground coriander
2 tsp ground cumin
1 tsp mixed herbs
2 tsp chilli powder
2 lbs/900g mixed veg, washed, trimmed and cut into good sized chunks e.g. peppers, turnips, carrots, mushrooms, leeks, celery and parsnips
14 oz/400g canned tomatoes, chopped
14 oz/400g canned kidney beans
14 oz/400g canned blackeye beans, drained and rinsed
½-¾ pint/300-450ml vegetable stock
1 tbsp tomato purée
4 fl oz/100ml red wine
Salt and freshly ground black pepper

Heat the oil and add the garlic, onion and fresh chilli. Cook gently until softened. Add the herbs and spices and stir over a gentle heat for a minute. Add the chopped vegetables, kidney and blackeye beans, stirring to coat in the spices. Add the chopped tomatoes, tomato purée, red wine, and about ½ pint/300ml of stock. Stir well, bring to the boil, cover and simmer for about 25-30 mins or until the vegetables are tender. Add more stock and spices if you think it needs it, during the cooking time. Season with salt and pepper.
    Serves 6.

Aubergines and mushrooms cooked in yogurt

This is a rich earthy stew, with curry spices and coriander. It is dense and muddy in colour, so serve it with a colourful rice, toned yellow with saffron.

1 onion, peeled and chopped
2 cloves garlic, crushed
1 red or green chilli, seeded and finely chopped
6 tbsp olive oil
1 tsp fennel seeds
1 tsp ground cumin
2 tsp ground coriander
2 medium sized aubergines, trimmed and diced into large cubes
8 oz/225g mushrooms, wiped and sliced
2 tomatoes, skinned and chopped
5 fl oz/150ml Greek yogurt
1 tsp garam masala
4 tbsp finely chopped fresh coriander
Salt and freshly ground black pepper

Heat the oil in a large heavy based pan, add the onion, garlic, and chilli and cook gently until softened. Stir in the spices, cook for a minute, then add the aubergine and mushrooms. Cook gently for 5 mins. Stir in the tomatoes and yogurt, cover and simmer for a further 20-25 mins until the vegetables are tender and the sauce is rich and thick. Stir in the fresh coriander, season to taste and serve hot.
    Serves 4.

Peperonata

This is what is often called Italian Ratatouille. A colourful dish of thinly sliced peppers, tomatoes and basil, gently stewed until tender. Serve it with a fresh pasta, flavoured with spinach or tomatoes, and drizzled with a fruity extra virgin olive oil.

2 tbsp olive oil
1 oz/30g butter
1 clove garlic, crushed
1 onion, thinly sliced
6 large ripe peppers — use red, yellow and green —
**   cored, seeded and sliced into thin strips**
6 large tomatoes, skinned and chopped or 14 oz/400g
**   canned tomatoes, drained and chopped**
2 tbsp fresh basil, finely chopped or 3 tsp dried basil
4 oz/115g grated fresh Parmesan
Salt and freshly ground black pepper

Heat oil and butter in large heavy based pan. Add the garlic and onion and sweat together for a few minutes. Add the peppers, cover and cook gently for 10-15 mins until soft, stirring occasionally. Add the chopped tomatoes and basil, and season. Cover and continue to simmer for 10-15 mins until excess liquid is cooked off and the peppers are very tender. Serve sprinkled with the Parmesan.
    Serves 3-4.

Blackeye bean and butternut stew

Butternut squash are excellent cooked in stews, retaining both their texture and vibrant orange colour. Serve this mildly spiced stew with fragrant Basmati rice or crusty garlic bread.

2 tbsp olive oil
2 cloves garlic, crushed
1 onion, peeled and roughly chopped
1 tsp ground cumin
1 tsp ground coriander
½ tsp chilli powder
1 large or 2 small butternut squash (about 2 lbs/900g),
   peeled, seeded and cubed
8 oz/225g mushrooms, thickly sliced
14 oz/400g canned tomatoes, chopped
14 oz/400g canned blackeye beans, drained and rinsed
Approx ¼ pint/150ml vegetable stock
2 tbsp fresh coriander, finely chopped
Salt and freshly ground black pepper

Crème fraiche or yogurt to serve

Heat oil in a heavy pan, add garlic and onion and sweat until softened. Stir in the spices and cook for a minute then add the squash and mushrooms, stirring to coat in the spices. Stir in tomatoes, beans, and a little stock. Bring to the boil, lower the heat and simmer, covered for 20-30 mins or until the squash is tender. Check during the cooking time that the stew isn't drying out, adding more stock if necessary. Season to taste, and just before serving, stir in the fresh coriander. Serve with the crème fraiche or yogurt.
   Serves 4.

BREADS, BLINIS AND PANCAKES

Cornmeal blinis

Blinis are a Russian-style yeasted pancake. They are usually made with buckwheat flour but here I've used cornmeal, which gives them a lovely golden colour and mildly nutty flavour. Serve them hot from the pan with soured cream, a fresh Ricotta cheese or just spread with butter.

4 oz/115g plain flour
4 oz/115g cornmeal (or polenta)
½ sachet 'easy-blend' dried yeast
½ tsp salt
3 eggs, separated
12 fl oz/350ml warmed milk
Olive oil or butter for frying

Combine the flour and cornmeal then place half in a separate bowl. Mix the yeast with half the flour and cornmeal, and stir in half the milk and the egg yolks, beaten, combining until smooth. Cover and leave in a warm place for an hour to prove. Stir in the remaining milk and flour, season with salt, cover and set aside for a further hour. When ready to cook, whisk the egg whites until stiff and fold into the batter. Heat a little olive oil or butter in a frying pan and add about 1 tbsp batter for each blini, cooking each side for 1-2 mins until lightly-browned and slightly risen. Serve immediately. Any excess batter can be covered and will keep for a couple of days in the fridge.
Makes 12-14 blinis.

Mozzarella and onion bread

This is a moist bread, fragrant with Mozzarella and basil, and topped with tender, stewed onions. It is best served hot or warm, alongside salads, pastas, or tomato-based stews.

For the dough
6 oz/170g plain flour
6 oz/170g wholemeal plain flour
2 tsp 'easy-blend' dried yeast
5 oz/140g Italian Mozzarella cheese, grated
2 tbsp finely chopped fresh basil
5 fl oz/150ml warm water
2 tbsp olive oil
1 tsp salt

For the topping
2 large onions, peeled and thinly sliced
2 tbsp olive oil

First make the dough, sift the flours into a large bowl, add the yeast, salt, basil and Mozzarella and stir to combine. Make a well in the centre and pour in the water and olive oil, mixing to a smooth dough. Turn onto a lightly-floured board and knead for 5-10 mins until smooth and elastic. Place in a lightly-oiled bowl, cover with cling film and leave in a warm place to rise for 1½-2 hours. While the bread is rising, heat the oil, add the onions, cover and cook gently, stirring occasionally for 30-40 mins, until browned and very tender. Salt lightly. When the dough has doubled in size punch it down and knead again for a couple of minutes. Place on a lightly-oiled baking sheet and flatten to a large round. Spread the onions over the dough and bake at gas mark 6, 200C/400F for 30-40 mins, until golden brown and crusty.
Makes 1 loaf.

Cornmeal and Gruyère pancakes

These are savoury pancakes with a grainy texture and mildly nutty flavour. They're lovely served hot, alongside a stew or spicy salsa, or just spread with butter or a mild, creamy Ricotta cheese.

4 oz/115g plain flour
6 oz/170g cornmeal (or polenta)
1 tsp baking powder
1 tsp bicarbonate of soda
1 tsp salt
1 oz/30g caster sugar
½ tsp paprika
2 oz/55g butter, melted
6 fl oz/175ml milk
2 eggs
3 oz/85g Gruyère cheese, grated
Olive oil or butter for frying

Combine the dry ingredients in a large bowl. Beat the eggs with the milk and stir in the melted butter. Pour into the cornmeal mixture and mix to a smooth batter. Stir in the cheese and set aside for 10 mins. Heat a little oil or butter in a frying pan and when it's hot, spoon the batter into the pan, allowing about a dessert spoon per pancake. Cook for a minute or two on each side until golden brown. Transfer the cooked pancakes onto a rack or keep warm in the oven while you cook the remaining batter, adding more oil or butter to the pan as needed. Makes 14-16 pancakes.
    Serves 6-8.

Pan bagnat

This is a crusty loaf, hollowed out, and filled with a mixture of grilled vegetables, herbs, olives and Mozzarella. It makes a lovely Mediterranean-style sandwich, sliced into thick wedges to reveal the colourful layers of the filling. Use a good quality loaf, and once filled, allow it to sit for a while before serving to let the flavours develop.

1 long, large crusty French or Italian loaf
6 tbsp extra virgin oil (plus extra for brushing
    the vegetables)
2 cloves garlic, crushed
2 tbsp fresh basil, finely chopped
1 large aubergine, sliced ¼ inch thick
1 red and 1 yellow pepper
4 ripe plum tomatoes, thinly sliced
20 green or black olives, pitted and sliced
6 oz/170g fresh or smoked Mozzarella cheese, thinly sliced

Cut the loaf in half by cutting across it, leaving the base and the top of the loaf and pull out most of the soft dough, leaving the crusts intact. Brush the aubergine slices and peppers with oil and place under a hot grill until the aubergine is soft and lightly-browned and the skins of the peppers have blackened. Transfer the peppers to a bowl and cover. When cool enough to handle, remove skins and slice the peppers. Brush the hollowed out crusts with the olive oil, sprinkle the garlic and basil over the base, and layer with the aubergine, peppers, tomatoes, cheese, and olives. Season with salt and pepper. Press on the top crust, wrap in tin foil and leave for a couple of hours, or longer, before serving. Makes 1 large sandwich.
    Serves 6-8.

Cornbread with garlic, chilli and coriander

A southern dish from America, cornbread makes the perfect accompaniment to spicy stews, especially those made with chilli. It is very easy and quick to make, using no yeast, being more like a batter. The resulting bread is soft and light but does not keep well, so use it all at once or freeze any leftovers. I've made it spicy in this recipe, but you could vary it by adding herbs such as basil or rosemary instead of the chillis and coriander.

4 oz/115g plain flour
4 oz/115g cornmeal or polenta
1½ tbsp caster sugar
2½ tsp baking powder
½ tsp salt
2 eggs
8 fl oz/250ml milk
2 oz/55g butter, melted
1 clove garlic, crushed
1 fresh chilli, seeded and finely chopped or 3 dried whole chillis, crumbled
3 tbsp fresh coriander, finely chopped
Freshly ground black pepper

Mix together the dry ingredients adding the chilli, garlic, coriander and some freshly ground black pepper. Beat the eggs in a bowl and stir in the melted butter and milk. Pour into the dry ingredients, mixing together well but quickly, so as not to overmix the batter. Pour into a buttered 10x6 inch/25x15cm or 8x8 inch/20x20cm baking pan and bake at gas mark 6, 200C/ 400F for about 30 minutes, until golden brown and firm to the touch. Cut into squares and serve warm from the oven. Makes 6-8 slices.
Serves 3-4.

Grilled polenta with Parmesan

Polenta is ground maize, the same as cornmeal, but usually coarser. In Italy it is served as an alternative to bread, cut into slices whilst hot or cold. I find it benefits from a bit of tarting up, and I add cheese and herbs then grill it which crisps up the outside, whilst leaving it soft and grainy inside. Serve instead of bread with any meal, particularly stews, pastas and Italian dishes.

10 oz/285g polenta (or coarse cornmeal)
2 pints/1.1 litres water
2 tsp salt
4 oz/115g freshly grated Parmesan
2 oz/55g butter
2 tbsp finely chopped fresh basil
Olive oil for brushing
Salt and freshly ground black pepper

In a large pan, bring the water to the boil and add the salt. Gradually whisk in the polenta, stirring all the time so that no lumps form. Cook over a gentle heat for about 20-25 mins, stirring all the time. This might seem laborious, but it's necessary to prevent it from sticking to the pan. Add more water if necessary, but keep the mixture thick. When cooked, remove from the heat and stir in the butter, cheese and basil. Season with salt and pepper. Transfer the polenta to a buttered tray, spread out and leave to harden. When cool, cut into squares about 3 inch/8cm across. Brush both sides with olive oil and place on an oiled tray under a hot grill. Cook on both sides until lightly browned.
   Serves 4-6.

Oatmeal and walnut pancakes with maple syrup

Pancakes and maple syrup are an American classic. This is a delicious variation, resulting in little oaty pancakes spiked with bits of crunchy walnut. Serve them hot and fresh, for a Sunday breakfast or brunch.

3 oz/85g oatmeal
4 oz/115g plain flour
½ tsp baking soda
½ tsp baking powder
½ tsp ground nutmeg
1 oz/30g soft brown sugar
1 egg, beaten
1 oz/30g butter, melted
10 fl oz/300ml milk
2 oz/55g walnuts, finely chopped
Sunflower oil for frying
Real maple syrup to serve (not maple-flavoured syrup
   which bears little resemblance)

Butter to serve

Sift together the flour, baking soda and baking powder. Stir in the oatmeal, sugar, and nutmeg then add the egg, milk and melted butter. Combine until the batter is smooth, then stir in the walnuts. Heat a little oil in a large, heavy based frying pan. When it's hot, add the batter, allowing about 1 tbsp per pancake. The batter is runny and will spread so do not cook too many at once. Cook until bubbles appear on the surface, and the underside is golden brown. Flip the pancakes and cook for a minute on the other side. Serve hot from the pan, dotted with a little butter and drizzled with maple syrup. Makes 10-12 pancakes.
   Serves 4-5.

Focaccia

Focaccia is a rustic flattish Italian bread, sprinkled with coarse sea salt and fragrant with olive oil. It's an easy bread to make, but you need to account for a fairly long rising time, so start the dough early in the day if you want it for an evening meal. Best eaten on the day it's made, hot or warm from the oven, spread with either plain or garlic butter. The bread can also be frozen, wrapped tightly in cling film.

6 oz/170g unbleached plain white flour
6 oz/170g plain wholemeal flour
1 sachet (2½ tsp) 'easy-blend' dried yeast
½ tbsp coarse sea salt (plus extra for topping)
1 tbsp fresh rosemary, finely chopped
2 tbsp olive oil (plus extra for brushing)
8-10 fl oz/250-300ml warm water

Measure the flours into a large bowl. Sprinkle on the yeast, salt and rosemary and mix well. Make a well in the centre and mix in the olive oil and enough water to combine to a soft dough. Turn it onto a lightly-floured surface and knead for 10 mins, then place in a lightly-oiled bowl, turning to coat. Cover with a damp tea towel and leave in a warm place to rise for 1½ hours, until doubled. Again on a lightly-floured surface, knead for a minute then roll out to a rough oval about ½ inch thick. Place on a lightly-oiled baking tray and either make diagonal slashes in the dough, or dimple it with your fingers. Cover and leave to rise again for 1½ hours. Heat oven to gas mark 6, 200C/400F for at least 30 mins before baking. Brush the dough with olive oil and sprinkle with 2 tsp sea salt. Bake for 25-35 mins until golden brown, spraying lightly with water twice in the first 10 mins to give a good crust.
Serves 6-8.

Cheese and herb bread

This makes a close-textured, savoury, flavoursome bread that is delicious with pâtés, cheeses, or as an accompaniment to soups. It's a moist bread that keeps well, and can be frozen.

12 oz/350g plain wholemeal flour
12 oz/350g bleached plain white flour
2 sachets 'easy-blend' active dried yeast
1 tbsp sugar
1 tbsp sea salt
2 tbsp mixed fresh herbs, finely chopped — use marjoram, basil and dill
4 oz/115g Gruyère cheese, grated
2 eggs, beaten
4 tbsp olive oil
10-12 fl oz/300-350ml warm water
1 egg, beaten with half tbsp milk, for egg wash

Mix together the flours in a large bowl. Stir in the yeast, sugar, salt, herbs and grated cheese. Mix in the eggs, oil, and enough water to bind to a soft dough. Knead the dough on a lightly-floured surface for 5-10 mins until smooth and glossy, adding only enough flour to keep the dough from sticking. Turn the dough into a lightly-oiled bowl turning to coat the top with oil. Cover with cling film or a damp tea towel and leave to rise in a warm place for 1½ hours, until doubled. Punch it down, knead again for a minute and let it rise again for about 30 mins. Divide the dough in half and shape into oiled loaf tins. Let the dough rise again in the tins for 30 mins. Preheat the oven to gas mark 4, 180C/350F. Brush the egg wash over the top of the loaves and bake for 50-60 mins until golden brown and crusty. Remove from tins and cool on a wire rack.
    Makes 2 loaves.

Cornmeal and sun-dried tomato bread

Studded with bits of chewy, sun-dried tomatoes, this bread is soft, dense and has a lovely grainy texture from the cornmeal. Sun-dried tomatoes are available either packed in oil or dried. The ones in oil tend to have a better flavour and texture, but if you can't get them, dried can be used. They need to be soaked in water for 20-30 minutes until softened, and then used in the same way. This bread is best served from the oven, although any leftovers can be frozen, or are good toasted.

6 oz/170g cornmeal or polenta
1 lb/450g unbleached strong white flour
1 sachet 'easy-blend' dried yeast
1 tsp salt
3 oz/85g butter, melted
5 floz/150ml warm water
5 fl oz/150ml milk
6-8 sun-dried tomatoes, packed in oil, thinly sliced and diced

To make the dough, sift the flour into a large bowl and stir in the cornmeal, salt and yeast. Make a well in the centre and pour in the butter, water and milk. Add the tomatoes and stir to form a firm dough. Turn onto a floured surface and knead for 8-10 mins until smooth and elastic. Turn into a lightly-oiled bowl, cover with cling film and leave in a warm place until doubled in volume, this should take about 1½ to 2 hours. When risen, punch it down and knead again for 5 mins. Place the dough in a lightly-oiled loaf tin or shape into a round on an oiled baking tray. Cover lightly and leave to rise again until doubled — a further 1-1½ hours. Bake in the oven preheated to gas mark 6, 200C/400F for 30-35 mins, until golden brown and crusty. Serve hot or warm from the oven.
    Makes 1 loaf.

Herb crêpes

Crêpes are thin French pancakes and are not difficult to make. If you haven't made them before it might just take a couple of trial runs to get them right. This is the basic crêpe batter with added herbs. They can be rolled around a filling, such as Peperonata (see page 103), or served with a salsa and sour cream. Once cooked, the crêpes can be frozen, interleaved with greaseproof paper, or the batter can be kept, covered, in the fridge for a couple of days.

4 oz/115g plain flour
Pinch of salt
2 large eggs
1 oz/30g melted butter or 1 tbsp olive oil
8 fl oz/250ml milk
2 tbsp finely chopped fresh herbs (basil, dill, rosemary,
     thyme or coriander)
Freshly ground black pepper and extra butter for cooking

Sieve flour and salt into a bowl, making a well in the centre. Beat the eggs together with the milk. Gradually add to the flour, mixing to a smooth batter. Stir in the butter or olive oil and mix in the herbs. Season with black pepper. Cover the batter and leave to rest for at least 30 mins before cooking. Using an omelette or pancake pan with shallow sides, heat a small knob of butter. Swirl to coat the pan, and when hot add a small ladleful of batter rolling the pan to spread out the mixture. Cook the crêpe quickly over a medium heat until golden brown on the bottom. Turn it over using a spatula and cook briefly on the other side. Makes 12-16 crêpes.
   Serves 4-5.

CAFE GANDOLFI, ALBION STREET — One of Glasgow's most popular cafes, the Gandolfi offers a varied, inventive, menu with a good deal of choice for vegetarians. The food is freshly-made on the premises, using Scottish produce whenever possible, and served in an environment which is friendly and relaxed.

CAKES AND DESSERTS

Carrot and pecan cake

Initially treated with scepticism as one of those weird, 'veggie' things, carrot cake is now commonplace and is available in many cafes, delicatessens, and supermarkets. There are, however, a lot of duff specimens about. The real thing should be very moist and dense-looking but have a light texture, the whole being topped off with fresh cream cheese icing. The best policy is always to make your own.

    8 fl oz/250ml sunflower oil
    6 oz/170g caster sugar
    3 large eggs
    2 fl oz/50ml maple syrup
    6 oz/170g plain flour
    1 tsp baking powder
    1 tsp baking soda
    8 oz/225g finely grated carrots
    4 oz/115g pecan nuts, roughly chopped
    1 tsp freshly grated root ginger

For the cream cheese icing
    2 oz/55g butter
    4 oz/115g cream cheese
    3 oz/85g icing sugar

Preheat oven to gas mark 4, 180C/350F. Place the oil and sugar in a mixer or food processor, beating until combined. Add the eggs, one at a time, beating until smooth and frothy, and beat in the maple syrup. Combine the flour with the baking soda and baking powder, and gradually beat into the liquid, mixing well until smooth. Stir in the carrots, ginger and pecans. Grease a 9-10 inch/23-25cm springform cake tin, and line with greaseproof paper, brushed with sunflower oil. Pour the mixture into the tin and bake for 50 minutes-1 hour, until a knife inserted in the centre comes out clean. Allow to cool slightly before removing from tin, and cool on a wire rack. For the icing, beat together the butter and cream cheese, then gradually beat in the icing sugar, mixing well until smooth and creamy. Spread over the cooled cake.

Serves 6-8.

VEGETARIAN ASHOKA, ELDERSLIE STREET — The original curry house is now closed, but it has relocated to the other side of the street and still serves the best curries in Glasgow — they just happen to be 100% meat free. The menu is extensive, the prices reasonable and the quality consistently good.

Ricotta and almond tart

An Italian-style dessert, with a crisp, biscuit pastry and creamy filling, flavoured with marsala, almonds, vanilla and lemon. Serve it warm or cold, either on its own, or with a little fresh cream or vanilla ice-cream.

For the pastry
    8 oz/225g plain flour
    2 oz/55g caster sugar
    4 oz/115g butter
    2 egg yolks
    A little milk

For the filling
    4 oz/115g sultanas
    4 tbsp marsala wine or dry sherry
    ½ vanilla pod, split lengthways
    1 egg
    2 oz/55g caster sugar
    2 oz/55g ground almonds
    12 oz/350g Ricotta cheese
    Juice and finely grated zest of 1 lemon
    2 oz/55g pine nuts, lightly toasted in a pan

First soak the sultanas in the marsala or sherry with the vanilla pod for at least 12, or preferably, 24 hours. For the pastry, rub the butter into the flour and sugar until crumbly. Stir in the egg yolks and combine until smooth, adding a little milk to bind the dough if necessary. Wrap the dough in cling film and leave to rest in the fridge for 30 minutes.

For the filling, beat the egg with the sugar until pale and thick. Stir in the ground almonds, Ricotta, lemon juice and zest, and mix well until smooth. Remove the vanilla pod from the sultanas, and stir the sultanas into the Ricotta mixture along with any excess soaking liquid. Roll out the pastry to line a 9-10 inch/23-25cm loose-bottomed tart tin. Prick the base with a fork and partially bake in oven gas mark 6, 200C/400F for 15 mins. Pour the filling into the partially baked pastry crust and sprinkle with the pine nuts. Return to oven and bake for 25-35 mins until lightly set and golden brown. Allow to cool slightly before removing from tin.

Serves 6-8.

Summer berry brûlée

This is a summery dessert of a light vanilla custard, baked over a layer of fresh, ruby berries. When berries are out of season, the dessert can be made with just the custard, resulting in a classic crème brûlée.

10 fl oz/300ml cream
½ vanilla pod, split lengthways
3 egg yolks
2 oz/55g caster sugar
4 oz/115g strawberries, washed, stemmed, and sliced
1-1½ tbsp brown sugar

Place the cream and vanilla pod in a pan and infuse over a very gentle heat for 15 minutes, stirring occasionally. Do not allow it to come to the boil. Beat together the egg yolks and caster sugar in a bowl. Remove the vanilla pod from the cream.

Scrape out the seeds, stirring them back into the cream, pour into the egg mixture and stir to combine. Return to the pan and stir over a gentle heat for a further 5 minutes, until the mixture coats the back of the spoon. Again, do not allow it to boil. Divide the fruit between four ramekins, about 4 ins/10cm round, and pour over the custard. Place the ramekins in a deep-sided baking tray, filled with enough water to come halfway up the sides of the dishes.

Bake in oven gas mark 4, 180C/350F for 25-30 minutes, until the custard is lightly set. Remove dishes from the baking tray and leave to cool. Heat the grill, sprinkle the custards with brown sugar, enough to cover evenly, and place under the hot grill until the sugar has melted and is starting to bubble — this will take just a couple of minutes, so watch it carefully in order not to let it burn. Cool again, then refrigerate for 2-3 hours before serving.

Serves 4.

Courgette and walnut cake

Just as carrots work well in a cake, so do courgettes, their flavour being subtle, almost impossible to identify. The end result is a cake which is delicately moist and light, and not overly sweet. It keeps well, and is actually nicer when served slightly chilled, so store it in a tin in the fridge.

8 fl oz/250ml sunflower oil
6 oz/170g caster sugar
3 large eggs
8 oz/225g plain flour
1 tsp baking powder
1 tsp bicarbonate of soda
½ tsp ground nutmeg
½ tsp salt
1 lb/450g courgettes, grated
4 oz/115g walnuts, roughly chopped

For the cream cheese icing
2 oz/55g butter
4 oz/115g cream cheese
3 oz/85g icing sugar

Preheat oven to gas mark 4, 180C/350F. Grease a 10-11 inch/ 25-28cm springform cake tin and line with lightly-oiled greaseproof paper. Place the oil and sugar in a mixer or food processor and combine until well-mixed. Add the eggs, one at a time, mixing well until frothy. Sift the flour with the baking powder, soda, salt and nutmeg. Add to the egg mixture, and combine until smooth and blended. Stir in the courgettes and walnuts, and pour into the prepared tin. Bake in the centre of the oven for 45-55 minutes, until a knife inserted in the centre comes out clean, and the cake is lightly browned. Allow to cool slightly before removing from tin, and cool on a wire rack. To make the icing, beat together the butter and cream cheese until smooth, and gradually beat in the icing sugar until pale and creamy. Spread over the cooled cake.
    Serves 8-10.

Blueberry cheesecake

The addition of Ricotta cheese makes this a lighter, less cloying cheesecake than those made wholly with cream cheese. Blueberries are perfect in this dessert, holding their shape and texture, but if they aren't available you could use other summer berries, or cubes of ripe fresh apricots, peaches, or nectarines.

For the base
8 oz/225g digestive biscuits, finely ground
4 oz/115g butter, melted

For the filling
8 oz/225g cream cheese
8 oz/225g Ricotta cheese
3 large eggs
4 oz/115g caster sugar
1 tsp vanilla essence
Finely grated zest of 1 lemon
8 oz/225g blueberries, washed and stemmed

Melt the butter in a pan, stir in the ground digestives and mix well. Press into the base of a greased 9 inch/23cm springform cake tin and chill in the fridge.

For the filling, beat together the cream cheese and Ricotta until smooth. Beat in the eggs, one at a time, then add the sugar, vanilla essence, and lemon rind, and beat well until smooth and creamy. Stir in the blueberries and pour the mixture over the base. Bake in oven gas mark 4, 180C/350F for 50 mins-1 hour, until set and lightly browned. Leave to cool, transfer onto a plate, and chill in the fridge for at least 3 hours before serving.

Serves 6-8.

Oatbran and walnut muffins

Either pinhead oatmeal or oatbran can be used for these muffins. Both are readily available, and add a slightly crumbly texture and a lovely nutty flavour. These are quick to make and are delicious served hot from the oven, spread with butter, honey, or cream cheese.

8 fl oz/250ml milk
6 oz/170g oatbran
2 eggs
3 oz/85g soft brown sugar
A few drops of vanilla essence
4 oz/115g butter, melted
4 oz/115g unbleached plain flour
3 oz/85g wholemeal plain flour
1 tbsp baking powder
1 tsp baking soda
½ tsp salt
2 eating apples, peeled, cored and grated
2 oz/55g walnuts finely chopped

Grease 12 good-sized muffin tins. Mix together the milk and oatbran and set aside. Beat the eggs with the sugar until light and smooth. Stir in the vanilla essence and melted butter. In another bowl, sieve the flours with the baking powder, baking soda and salt, and stir in the apples and walnuts. Combine the oatbran with the egg mixture, then stir in the dry ingredients. Be careful not to over-mix the batter, as this would cause the muffins to be heavy. Spoon into the muffin tins and bake in oven gas mark 6, 200C/400F for 20-25 mins until well-risen, golden brown and just firm to the touch. Allow to cool for a few minutes before removing from tins.
   Makes 12 muffins.

Festive ice-cream

The addition of dried fruits soaked in brandy give this ice-cream a rich flavour, one which is ideally suited to the festive season. They can easily be omitted, in which case the ice-cream will be a more traditional, but equally delicious, vanilla. If you are using the fruits, allow plenty of time for soaking to let the flavours develop.

8 oz/225g mixed dried fruits (apricots, figs and prunes)
4 fl oz/100ml brandy
6 fl oz/175ml milk
9 fl oz/275ml double cream
4 egg yolks
3 oz/85g caster sugar
2 oz/55g pistachio nuts, finely chopped
½ vanilla pod, split or 1 tsp vanilla essence

Chop the fruits, removing stones from the prunes and stems from the figs. Place in a bowl, pour over the brandy, cover and leave to soak for at least 4 hours. The longer the better, so try to leave for about 24 hours. To make the ice cream, gently heat together the milk, cream and vanilla. Whisk the egg yolks with the sugar until pale and thick. When the milk is about to boil, whisk into the egg yolks. Return to the pan and cook gently, do not allow to boil. Stir carefully until the mixture coats the back of the spoon. This should take just a couple of minutes.

Pour into a bowl, cover and leave to cool. If using a vanilla pod, remove it when cooled, but scrape the seeds out and mix them into the custard. Using a food processor or mixer, whisk the custard until starting to go frothy, then pour back into the bowl and freeze for an hour or two until it is firming up.

Whisk again until thickening and frothy, return to the freezer and leave to firm again. Continue in this way until it whisks to a smooth, creamy, thick mixture and has doubled in volume. This might take three or four whiskings. After the last whisking, stir in the soaked fruit and nuts. Return to freezer and freeze for 4 hours until firm, remembering to take it out and beat it a couple of times before it begins to firm up in order to distribute the fruit and nuts. This will keep in the freezer compartment for up to two weeks.

Serves 6.

INDEX